BOOKKEE...

&

QUICKBOOKS

2 IN 1

A Beginner's Guide to Accounting and
Bookkeeping for Small Business

BY MICHAEL KANE

By reading this document, the reader agrees that under no circumstances are the author responsible for any losses, direct or indirect, which are incurred as a result of the use of the information contained within this document, including, but not limited to, —errors, omissions, or inaccuracies.

Table of Contents

BOOKKEEPING

A Beginner's Guide to Accounting and Bookkeeping For Small Businesses

BY MICHAEL KANE

INTRODUCTION

The word bookkeeping and accounting are accounting terminologies. If you are an accountant, business owner, business administrator, etc. you should understand what these terms mean. Bookkeeping and accounting are very important aspects of business activities. Although some people use these two terms, interchangeably, accounting, and bookkeeping have different meanings.

If you want to run a small business, you need to have an understanding of bookkeeping and accounting. Bookkeeping and accounting have a lot of benefits for small business owners. A successful small business is the result of accurate bookkeeping and accounting, and understanding the practices of bookkeeping is very important for the smooth operation of your business.

The practices of accounting and bookkeeping are not difficult to understand. This is the ultimate guide to bookkeeping and accounting for beginners. It explains everything you need to understand these subjects.

Several small businesses do well in sales, advertising, building good teams, and customer services. However, these businesses have issues when it comes to the aspect of bookkeeping and accounting. A business will run well if transactions are recorded, and different types of accounts are kept properly.

BOOKKEEPING

You can only evaluate the performance of your businesses if you practice the art of bookkeeping and accounting. Bookkeeping and accounting help organize your finances and evaluate your business's performance. As a business owner, you must have a financial understanding of how your business operates.

A good bookkeeping and accounting system helps you to plan for the future. As a small business owner, you can decide to do your bookkeeping yourself or hire someone to help you do it. The primary aspect of the accounting system in an organization is bookkeeping.

Some people underrate the importance of bookkeeping in businesses. The art of bookkeeping keeps your business on the right track. If you do not understand the bookkeeping and accounting system, your business might fail. With an effective bookkeeping and accounting system, you will understand and plan your business.

If you are willing to learn the art of bookkeeping, this book will help you achieve your goal. Bookkeeping and accounting will help you to keep a good track of your sales, purchases, expenses, profits, bad debts, etc. One of the keys to operating a successful business is effective bookkeeping and accounting.

Regardless of the type of business you are operating, the accounting and bookkeeping requirements are the same.

When it comes to accounting and bookkeeping, you need to decide the accounting software you'd like to use, the accounting method suitable for you, understand how transactions are recorded, and establish different types of accounts.

You need to ask yourself some questions before you start managing your business. Questions like: "How will I record my transactions?" "What type of accounting software should I opt for?" "Can I manage my business myself or hire someone to do it for me?" "What kind of accounting method should I use?"

Bookkeeping and accounting system can be very engaging and stressful if you do not understand the basics of bookkeeping and accounting. Knowing the right thing to do is one of those things that will help you run a successful business. There are different aspects of bookkeeping you need to learn for the smooth running of your business.

Keeping up-to-date financial records of your small business makes you know how your business is fairing and what steps need to be taken for improvement. Effective bookkeeping shows how you can manage your business. The financial performance of your business helps to evaluate the success of your business.

Bookkeeping and accounting systems can be seen as a report card. A student's report card at the end of the term reveals the overall performance of that student; this is the same function of bookkeeping and accounting in small businesses. You can only perform better when you are aware of previous performance.

Why Businesses are Successful

There is no doubt that an effective bookkeeping and accounting system is the key to running a successful business. The art of bookkeeping and accounting systems is to understand the financial aspects of your business. A business will fail if it doesn't maintain good records of its transactions. A business can do well in all other aspects, but if it fails in its financial aspects, such a business will crumble.

The success of a business is determined by several factors, of which bookkeeping and accounting is a very important one. Success in business is not determined by how many sales you made or the profit you generated but by how you kept track of your transactions. The question is, how will you realize the profits generated and the sales you made if you do not keep records of your transactions?

It is only when you keep up-to-date financial records of your transactions that you can determine the performance of your business. A business is operated to generate profit, but this goal can be hindered if one fails to maintain an effective bookkeeping and accounting system.

The art of bookkeeping is an essential aspect of a business. Some small businesses failed - not because they did not make sales, or they failed to produce good products - but they failed to maintain an effective bookkeeping and accounting system.

We do not just emphasize the importance of bookkeeping and accounting because we want to force business owners to do it. The importance of bookkeeping and accounting is explained because it is vital for becoming a successful business owner and is important for both small and large businesses.

No matter how small your business is, you need to keep good track of all transactions. When you operate a business, you will certainly carry out some transactions, and these transactions should not be left unrecorded. This book was written to explain how to appropriately track those transactions.

Businesses operate well when effective bookkeeping and accounting systems are managed. To understand the art of bookkeeping, one needs to understand some basic concepts. A business should be operated to achieve success, not only to make a profit.

The Difference Between Accounting and Bookkeeping

Although the two concepts have been explained above, one needs to explain these two concepts broadly. When we talk about bookkeeping, we mean the day-to-day records of financial transactions carried out in a business or organization. Bookkeeping is an aspect of financial accounting. Most financial statements or reports are derived from bookkeeping.

Accounting involves summarizing financial transactions that have already been recorded. The primary goal of accounting is the preparation of financial reports or statements. There are different branches of accounting; these include management accounting, cost accounting, auditing, etc.

Accounting deals with summarizing bookkeeping results in annual financial reports. Bookkeeping is the fundamentals of accounting. This simply means that without bookkeeping, there will be nothing accounted for. Bookkeeping keeps track of financial transactions that all financial statements and reports are derived from.

Bookkeeping involves determining and recording financial transactions, preparing ledger accounts, and making trial balances. Accounting involves identifying, recording, and summarizing financial transactions, preparing financial reports, and analyzing financial statements. Financial accounting helps business owners, stakeholders, and investors to determine the financial position of an organization.

Bookkeeping is carried out according to the accounting conventions and concepts. Financial statements are not part of the bookkeeping process; they are derived from bookkeeping by accountants. Bookkeeping is performed by a bookkeeper, while a well-skilled accountant performs accounting. Bookkeeping and accounting are two different concepts, although they are related.

The Role of a Bookkeeper

A bookkeeper performs the following roles:

- Makes journal entries for all business transactions carried out.

- Prepares a trial balance.

- Records the inflow and outflow of cash in a business.

- Maintains and balances general ledgers, subsidiaries, and historical accounts.

- Responsible for preparing bank reconciliations.

- Issues invoices to debtors.

- Files tax returns.

- Ensures compliance with accounting principles.

- Serves as the middleman between a business and its customers.

- Pay accounts on the business's behalf.

Bookkeepers work in various organizations. Bookkeepers do not necessarily need to acquire formal education. To be a successful bookkeeper, you need to be knowledgeable about bookkeeping skills and major financial topics.

How to Run a Successful Small Business

Running a successful business is the topmost priority of small business owners. A business becomes successful not only because of the capital used for starting the business but the strategies and critical decisions made in the business. Below are tips on how you can run a successful business.

- Set up a trading strategy

A trading strategy is like an outline that shows the criteria for money management in a business. Technological advancement has made this easier for businesses today. You can evaluate a business idea before taking the risk with your capital. This is also referred to as back-testing.

This method helps business owners to decide if a business plan will work for a business.

Once you have a business plan and you have tested its feasibility, and it reveals positive results, then you can use the plan in your business. Ensure that you stick to the business plan you have designed for your business.

• Utilize the Internet to your advantage

There are so many businesses in the world. Your business is not the only one that exists as there are several businesses similar to yours. You can make use of technology like the Internet to get more business strategies and understand what will work for your type of business. By getting the necessary information from the Internet and using it to your advantage, this is a way of promoting your business.

Information is key. Business owners should learn more every day. It is very important that you understand what the markets need and then deliver exactly what they want. Good research enables small business owners to know facts about businesses.

• Establish a trading strategy based on facts

As a business owner, you can take your time to set up a business strategy that is based on known facts. Nobody wants to build his or her business based on myths. Do not be in a hurry to achieve your plans, but take it slowly.

CHAPTER 1

BASICS OF BOOKKEEPING

You must have heard of the word bookkeeping on one or two occasions. In the business world, bookkeeping is not a new thing. It has existed for so long. When we talk about bookkeeping, the first thing that comes to people's minds is that bookkeeping is the art of keeping books.

Bookkeeping is different from that; it is a broad terminology in financial accounting that entails the process of keeping good records of all financial transactions in a business. This chapter explains what bookkeeping is about.

What is Bookkeeping?

Bookkeeping is an accounting concept that refers to the act of recording, verifying, retrieving, storing, and organizing the financial transactions carried out in a business or organization. Bookkeeping is sometimes called record keeping. Bookkeeping is an aspect of financial accounting that deals with recording financial transactions and events in a business or organization.

Bookkeeping can be carried out manually or with the use of bookkeeping software. The principles of financial accounting lie in keeping accurate and up-to-date records. Therefore, bookkeeping is the basis of financial accounting. It is the source of information for most of the accounting systems.

Bookkeepers are trained to use their analytical skills in recording financial transactions because most accounting information is sourced from these financial records. There are different aspects of financial accounting; these include bookkeeping, auditing, share valuation, financial forecasting, etc. Without bookkeeping, none of these aspects can function; bookkeeping is the backbone of financial accounting.

Bookkeeping provides well-detailed and accurate information from which other accounts like balance sheets, trading, profit and loss accounts, ledgers, and depreciation, among others, are prepared. Without bookkeeping, none of these accounts can be prepared. Bookkeeping is a vital aspect of financial accounting.

Each financial transaction in a business must be recorded. There are ways in which these transactions are recorded. Bookkeeping does not only involve the recording of figures, but it also records financial transactions and events. Bookkeeping is essential for a business to thrive.

The concepts of bookkeeping and accounting are often used interchangeably, although they are separate. Bookkeeping is a vital aspect of accounting, while accounting is the general way of managing a business's finances. A person who studies bookkeeping is referred to as a bookkeeper.

A bookkeeper must understand some accounting principles and how transactions should be recorded. The process of recording and organizing transactions is called bookkeeping. Accounting is a broader concept and should not be mistaken for bookkeeping. Bookkeeping is simply an aspect of financial accounting.

Gone are the days when bookkeeping was done manually, the process of recording and organizing financial transactions has been made easier in today's world. Bookkeeping can be carried out via computer software. There are several programs used for recording and organizing transactions.

Keeping accurate and up-to-date records of all transactions is vital in bookkeeping. Bookkeeping is useless if the transactions recorded are not accurate. The most important factor in bookkeeping is accuracy.

Bookkeeping is done to offer well-detailed and accurate information required to create accounting statements.

The Importance of Bookkeeping

Bookkeeping is very important in small businesses. Bookkeeping is a core aspect of accounting. It is important in all businesses and organizations regardless of the type or size of businesses operated. Businesses can fail because of poor bookkeeping. Below are the reasons why bookkeeping is important.

Organization

When bookkeeping is defined, the word organization is used. Bookkeeping deals with the recording and the organizing of transactions. The organization is very important when running a business. A successful business owner is one that is very organized in all activities carried out.

Bookkeeping helps you gain access to the necessary details regarding your business. For instance, if you need some details about sales, an effective bookkeeping system will help you get the necessary information you need. Some parties, like employees, Internal Revenue Service, customers, lenders, researchers, auditors, and investors, are interested in your financial records. Providing these parties with accurate and well-detailed information can help your business.

The Internal Revenue Service can penalize you, as a business owner, if you refuse to provide the required, necessary records. Investors may stop investing in your business if they lack access to your records. Staying organized and up to date with your bookkeeping will help maintain a good working relationship between you and your investors.

An effective bookkeeping system will help you have access to the necessary information required from your business. If you are disorganized with your records, this can cause a big problem for you. Book organization is very important if you want a smooth running business.

Decision Making

If you want to make wise decisions in your business, then you need to practice effective bookkeeping. Bookkeeping helps you to make better decisions in your business. As a business owner, you need to make good decisions that will have a positive effect on your business. A bad decision can ruin your business and leave you with no choice than to shut down your business.

Decision making is a vital aspect of a business. You cannot make good decisions if you don't know anything about bookkeeping. Bookkeeping reveals areas where a business is lagging. With this information, you can set new goals to fix the problems in these areas.

To make a good decision, you need to know the necessary details that will help your business. Some businesses crumble because of bad decisions. If you keep good track of records in your business, you can make decisions based on these accurate and up to date records.

Budget Creation

A budget is necessary for all businesses and organizations. Even a country creates financial budgets yearly. A budget is a financial statement that shows the estimated income and expenditure. It is a way of creating a financial plan on how you will spend money. A budget helps you to plan for the future.

Creating a budget is very important for your business. When you have a correct estimate of expenses and income, it will help your business perform well. Creating a budget helps you make good plans. Carrying out efficient bookkeeping will help you create feasible budgets.

Good Planning

Good planning is an important practice in bookkeeping. Bookkeeping reveals the past performance of a business or organization, and by evaluating this, proper planning can be made for the future.

Bookkeeping helps you create strategic plans that will help your business. Bookkeeping helps you to plan for taxation. It also provides the necessary details to categorize expenses and revenues to help estimate future costs and profit.

Bookkeeping helps your certified public accountant determine which expenses are more favorable. For instance, providing lunch during conferences in your organization can be favorable to your business in terms of taxation.

Taxation

Every year, your business will most likely have to pay tax. Most businesses do not have accurate records, so the tax filing process is inefficient. With an efficient bookkeeping system, your financial details can be ready for tax filing.

During tax filing, bookkeeping provides your accountant with what is required for filing taxes. Accountants prepare tax reports to determine the tax payable to local and federal authorities. Accountants can only prepare tax reports with the help of an efficient bookkeeping system.

Profit Realization

Bookkeeping helps you to realize the profits you make in your business. For instance, bookkeeping records the income you generate in your business, and the income statement is derived from your bookkeeping. Calculating the profits made from your business helps you know the performance of your business.

Bookkeeping helps you to track the growth of your business. The amount of profit you realize from your business shows how your business is fairing. The trading, profit and loss account is derived from income and expenditure accounts in bookkeeping.

Good Reporting to Investors

Investors need accurate details of your business' financial transactions because they have a stake in the business. Investors have rights in your business and can make certain decisions. They need to know how their money is utilized, if the business is realizing profits or not, and what is needed to be done to improve the business.

Bookkeeping reveals all these things. With a good bookkeeping system in practice, your investors will have a clear picture of your business. The profit and loss account, which is obtained through bookkeeping, reveals the income generated and the loss incurred in the business. Bookkeeping helps you to give accurate reports to your investors.

Good Financial Management

The importance of bookkeeping can never be underestimated. It helps business owners maintain good cash flow. As a business owner, bookkeeping helps you take charge of the finances in your business. Bookkeeping analyzes your business' finances to ensure they are being managed properly. The only way to determine the overall performance of your business is by keeping good records of all financial transactions.

With bookkeeping, you can make balance sheets, trial balance, trading, ledger, profit, and loss accounts. The performance of a business can only be evaluated by making a comparison between these accounts.

Peace of Mind

One problem faced by business owners is how to practice effective and accurate bookkeeping. With an effective bookkeeping system in place, you'll have nothing to worry about if your records are requested by the IRS. You will not be scared when your investors, clients, the IRS, or banks ask for your financial statement. With a sound bookkeeping system, you do not need to have sleepless nights again.

Easy Auditing

If you maintain an effective bookkeeping system, your auditors will be grateful to you. Keeping good records of your transactions makes auditing as simple as ABC. If your books are well organized, auditing will be made easier and faster.

Auditors require certain documents from you, and if you cannot figure out where these documents are, your auditors can become frustrated. For instance, if your business is being audited by the Internal Revenue Service and your books are disorganized, you can be penalized.

Types of Bookkeeping

There are two major types of bookkeeping: single entry and double entry.

Single-Entry Bookkeeping

Small businesses mostly utilize the single-entry system of bookkeeping. It is easy and simple to carry out. Due to its simple nature, it is typically used for uncomplicated and small transactions. This system of bookkeeping keeps records of business expenses, cash sales, and profits.

Businesses having many capital transactions accounts receivable, and accounts payable do not utilize this system of bookkeeping. The single-entry system allows you to view all the expenses incurred and the income generated for a period. This system of bookkeeping is suitable for sole proprietors.

In the single-entry system of bookkeeping, there is only one entry for every transaction carried out. You record all entries in a column. In this system, you can prepare a two-column ledger, in which one is for expenses, and the other is for revenue. This system of bookkeeping does not record accounts such as accounts receivable, inventory, and the likes.

The single-entry can be used to calculate the profits realized in a business. Transactions in the single-entry system do not have a debit and credit side. This system of bookkeeping can make it difficult to trace revenue and expenses since they are all recorded in just one entry.

Double-Entry System

Both small and big businesses use the double-entry system of bookkeeping. The double entry system is sometimes call a "T-account" because the entries take on the shape of the letter "T" on the page. In the double-entry system, there are two columns for every account. There are two separate entries for every transaction carried out. There is a column for the debit account and another column for the credit account.

This system of bookkeeping is utilized by businesses that have complex transactions, organizations, or businesses that have accounts receivable, accounts payable, and inventory. Any income received is recorded on the debit side of the account, while expenses are recorded on the credit side of the account.

For example, if a customer pays you, it is recorded as income and also recorded in the account of the customer. If a transaction is carried out, you need to know which transaction is an income and which is an expense.

If an organization needs to pay a creditor, two accounts will be opened, the cash account and the customer's account. If you want to keep a check of your liability accounts, you need to utilize the double-entry system. In this system, a business owner can easily calculate the loss and profit of the organization. It also makes it easy to make financial statements directly from the books.

CHAPTER 2

TIPS ON BOOKKEEPING FOR SMALL BUSINESS

Small businesses need bookkeeping and accounting for their smooth running. No matter how small your business is, you need bookkeeping and accounting. Most small business owners manage their accounting systems themselves.

Small business accounting is easy and simple to do. There are small businesses that practice efficient bookkeeping and accounting systems. This chapter discusses the basics of small business accounting and what you need to do if you are a small business owner.

Steps on Small Business Bookkeeping

There are certain things you need to know and certain steps that need to be followed when operating small business accounting.

Understand Business Accounts

In small business accounting, all transactions carried out are recorded in different accounts. As a business owner, you need to know that there are five types of accounts. These accounts are equity, liabilities, expenses, assets, and revenues.

- Equity: This refers to the amount remaining after your liabilities have been subtracted from your assets.

- Liabilities: Liabilities are debts or financial obligations owed by an organization or business. Examples of liabilities are loans, accounts payable, customer deposits, etc.

- Expenses: Expenses are also called expenditures. They refer to the outflow of cash from businesses to acquire items or pay for services. Examples are the payment of utilities, salaries, etc.

- Assets: These are known to be resources and cash a business owns. These resources have economic value that later on provides financial benefit for a business. Examples are real estate, supplies, inventory, etc.

- Revenue: Revenue is also known as income. This refers to the in-flow of cash in a business; it is usually obtained through sales.

Accounting and bookkeeping start by creating the necessary accounts to record each transaction. You need to understand the accounts explained above very well before you start recording transactions in your business.

Open a Business Account

You need to open a bank account. This is very important since you now understand the various types of accounts in financial accounting. In the old days, a book known as a general ledger was used to record charts of accounts. These days, most organizations utilize different computer software to keep track of accounts. It can be a hard copy or virtual record; it is still regarded as the general ledger.

The cheapest software to use is spreadsheet software. A general ledger can be created using three methods: desktop accounting bookkeeping software, spreadsheet software, and cloud-based bookkeeping software. Desktop bookkeeping is good bookkeeping software that requires an up-front fee.

If you are utilizing cloud-based bookkeeping software like Wave, QuickBooks Online, you need to subscribe monthly, but the subscription is not as expensive as desktop software. You should open your business accounts to keep good records of all of your financial transactions.

Choose your Preferred Bookkeeping Method

There are different methods of bookkeeping. You can decide to use software for your bookkeeping or do it manually. You can use the single-entry or double-entry bookkeeping system. You can hire a professional to record your transactions, or you can do it yourself.

Before you start bookkeeping, you need to decide the best bookkeeping system you would like to practice. If you are operating a small business, the single-entry bookkeeping is ideal for you. However, the most common bookkeeping system used is double-entry bookkeeping. In the double-entry bookkeeping system, any transaction recorded in an account needs to be recorded in another account as an opposite entry.

In this system of bookkeeping, for every transaction, you are required to record two entries. There is always a debit (Dr) and a credit (Cr) column for all entries. The debit is always on the left side while the credit occupies the right side.

A double-entry bookkeeping system requires more tasks than single-entry bookkeeping. With this system, your books will be balanced, provided that you keep accurate and up-to-date records. It easier for you to know how much profit you realize if you use the double-entry bookkeeping system.

Record all Financial Transactions

The business accounts you created are not for fun; they are used for recording every financial transaction you carry out. After creating your business accounts and you have chosen the system of bookkeeping you want, the next step is to ensure you record all financial transactions properly.

An efficient bookkeeping system is one that contains well-detailed and up-to-date transactions. If you fail to record every financial transaction, then your bookkeeping is not efficient. Make sure you record each credit and debit transaction in the right column. If you fail to do this, your balances will not tally, and you cannot close your books.

If you are recording a transaction, the first thing you do is determine which account should be recorded on the debit side and the credit side. For instance, you purchased a new vehicle for your business for $20,000 and paid for it in cash. Two accounts will be opened: a cash account and equipment account. Since your cash is decreasing and your equipment is increasing, you will debit your equipment account and credit the cash account.

Close your Books

You must close your book at the end of the month or year. Balancing your books will help you determine your profits and where you need to make certain adjustments.

Your errors will be revealed if you are the type that keeps inaccurate information. The total of debits and credit accounts must tally when you are balancing your books.

If your books are well balanced, it shows that you have recorded all financial transactions properly. If the debit and credit side have different values, you'll have to go through your journal entries to locate the errors.

Make Financial Reports

If your books are well balanced, then you can make financial statements or reports from your books. Most financial statements like balance sheet, cash flow statement, profit, and loss statement are all derived from bookkeeping.

Making financial reports enables you to evaluate the financial performance of your business. The profit and loss statement, which is also known as an income statement, helps you to know how much profit realized or loss incurred in your business. It reveals the in-flow and out-flow of cash to and from your business.

The cash flow statement is just like the Profit and Loss account; it excludes non-cash items like depreciation. Cash flow statements reveal the aspect your business is spending on and where it is earning income. Bookkeeping helps you to make financial statements, and these statements can help you make financial decisions.

Store your Records Securely

Recording all financial transactions properly helps small businesses and makes it much easier to create financial records and reports. Keep your records in a secure place. You do not want a situation where you have to start looking for your records.

If you do not know about the principles of financial accounting, you can hire a professional to help you keep good records of your transactions. Ensure all your books are kept safely to prevent future problems and make sure you have backups.

The Fundamentals of Small Business Accounting

Every business needs to keep good records of its financial transactions to evaluate its overall performance on a yearly or monthly basis. There are certain principles you need to understand about small business accounting.

Accounting is a much broader concept that entails recording financial transactions and creating financial statements. Below are certain things you need to understand when operating small business accounting.

Open a Bank Account

As a business owner, you need to open a bank account where you will keep your business income. You cannot hold all your income as cash; you need to put some in your bank account. If you create a separate bank account for your records, it will make your work easier for you during tax filing.

Businesses like partnerships, corporations, and LLCs are required to hold a separate bank account. Sole proprietors do not need to operate a separate account. Open bank accounts that will make it easy for you to plan for taxes and organize funds.

For example, you can create a savings account and spend a proportion of each payment as your tax. Limited liability companies and corporations are legally required to operate a separate account and utilize a separate credit card to prevent mixing up personal and business assets.

Ensure you use your business name to open your business account. Ensure you open a bank account for your business, and your business should be registered with your province or state.

Use a Bookkeeping System

Bookkeeping is different from accounting. It entails the recording of day-to-day transactions carried out in a business or organization. Accounting is a much broader concept that evaluates business performance and translates the data recorded by a bookkeeper into financial statements.

As a business owner, you need to know the bookkeeping method that is favorable to you. You can utilize the accrual or cash method. In the cash method, all expenses and revenues are recorded at the time you receive the income or pay for expenses. While the accrual method records revenues and expenses immediately the transaction occurs, revenues and expenses are recorded even if you have not received payment.

Record your Expenses and Revenues

If you want to keep good records and determine your business's progress, you need to learn how to track your income and expenses. It helps you track the progress of your business, make financial reports, prepare tax returns, and keep records of deductible expenses.

Set up a system for recording receipts and other important accounts. You should always pay attention to receipts like meals and entertainment, vehicle-related expenses, home office receipts, travel receipts, and receipts for gifts. Make sure these receipts are carefully recorded.

Set Up Sales Tax Procedures

As a business owner, you need to set up sales tax procedures. These days, sales tax has been added to most products. When selling to international clients, you might not need to charge sales tax. Set up your sales tax procedures accounting for your state or province.

Sales taxes vary by state and city. When you sell products, you need to charge your customers' sales tax. Before you charge sales tax in any province or state, you need to apply to charge sales tax and report the sales tax in the state you intend to do so.

Prepare for Some Expenses

It is normal for businesses to pay for unforeseen expenses. No matter how carefully you have created a balance sheet and maintain cash flow reports, you cannot predict some expenses. It is always nice to know you planned for unforeseen expenditures.

You can save an emergency fund in case there's an emergency. Keeping a separate emergency fund can help you pay unplanned expenses. Avoiding running into debt in your business will help you realize more profits.

Keep Vital Bookkeeping Records

As a business owner, you should keep important bookkeeping records. Keep documents like bills, sales receipts, tax returns, customer invoices, canceled checks, bank statements, 1099 forms, deposit slips, and payroll documentation.

Be sure and store bookkeeping records as a protected file on your computer and backed up, either on a hard drive or in the cloud. It is also a good idea to keep hard copies of these files in a safe place in your office.

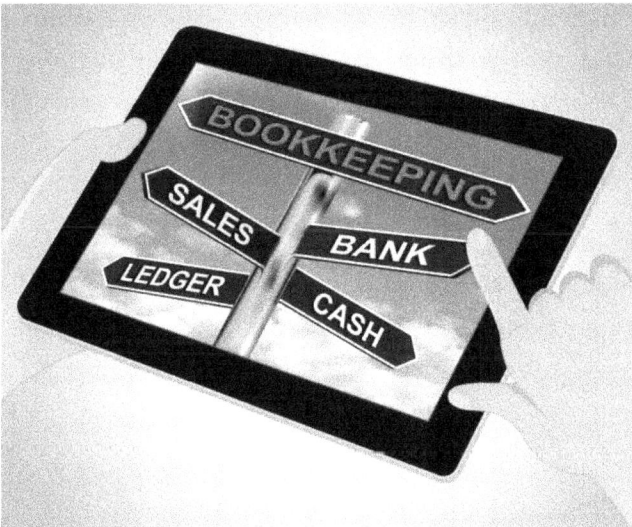

CHAPTER 3

ACCRUAL METHOD VS. CASH BASIS METHOD

What are the Two Methods of Accounting?

One of the decisions you need to make before you start bookkeeping in your small business is choosing the right method for your business. The two major methods of bookkeeping are the accrual and the cash basis method.

Cash Basis Accounting

In the cash basis method, income is received and recorded immediately you render a service or sell a product. This method of accounting does not accept or record accounts payable or accounts receivable.

Most small businesses use the cash basis method because it has a simple approach. It is easy and simple to know if a transaction has been carried out, and you don't need to record payables or receivables. The cash basis method helps you to keep track of the amount of cash your business has at a particular period.

Pros:

Simple to operate: The cash basis method is a simple bookkeeping process that makes it easy to track your money. This accounting method is ideal for small businesses or organizations that do not deal with big inventory.

Convenient and reliable: This method of accounting is known for its reliability and convenience. With the cash basis accounting method, it is easy to keep track of your expenses and revenues.

Income taxes: If you are using this method, you are not required to pay taxes on any income that has not been received. For example, if you sold a product to a customer for $500 in November and you don't receive payment until March, you don't pay taxes until you have received the payment in March.

Cons:

- It does not track accounts payable or receivable.

- It gives an unclear financial picture.

- It does not abide by the Generally Accepted Accounting Principles.

Accrual Basis Accounting

In this method, expenses and revenues are recorded when they are incurred or generated, irrespective of when the payment is received. For instance, in the accrual basis method, revenue will be recorded when a transaction has been completely carried out and not when you receive payment. This method is more common than the cash basis method.

One disadvantage of using this method is that you cannot track the in-flow and out-flow of cash properly. This method of accounting is more complicated than cash basis accounting. In this method, you record transactions before you close your books for the month. This method keeps track of accounts receivable and accounts payable.

Pros:

Gives a clearer financial picture: This method gives a clearer financial picture of your business and shows a better idea of expenses and income incurred and earned during a financial period.

Conforms to GAAP: The accrual method of accounting abides by the Generally Accepted Accounting Principles, which is the main reason it is recommended for companies earning over $25 million annually.

Cons:

- It is more complex than the cash basis method.

- It is not ideal for small businesses.

- Comparing the two accounting methods

In the cash basis method, income is received and recorded immediately you render a service or sell a product. The cash basis method of accounting records transactions when cash is received. This method of accounting does not accept or record accounts payable or accounts receivable.

In the cash basis method, expenses and revenues are recorded when they are incurred or generated irrespective of when payment is received. In the accrual basis method, revenue will be recorded when a transaction has been completely carried out and not when you receive payment.

Which Method of Accounting is Suitable for Small Businesses?

According to the Internal Revenue Service, the accrual method is recommended for businesses that earn over

$25 million on average. The Accrual method is suitable for corporations. The accrual method is used by corporations when reporting financial results or bookkeeping.

For small businesses, the cash basis method is recommended because of its simple nature. The choice of the accounting method to use is determined by the resources available, your business objectives, and the financial requirements of your business. However, the IRS advises that organizations must use the same method of accounting to report taxable income annually.

The cash basis method is ideal for small businesses that do not have inventory. If your business has a large inventory, the accrual method is ideal for you. For any business or organization that wants to change the methods of accounting, such a business is required to obtain approval from the Internal Revenue Service.

The accounting method you opt for influences the way you keep track of expenses and incomes on your financial statements. The Internal Revenue Service advises that businesses should utilize a consistent and effective accounting method. If you fail to be consistent with your accounting method, your tax returns will not be accepted by the IRS. Therefore, your business or organization may be penalized or fined.

Types of Bookkeeping Accounts

There are different accounts in bookkeeping. As a small business owner, you should know these accounts and understand how to record transactions in each of these accounts. You need to understand everything about your transactions. There are different types of accounts for small business bookkeeping. This section explains the different types of accounts in bookkeeping and how they are managed.

Sales

The sales account records all revenue generated from what you sell. All businesses generate sales by selling an item or product or by rendering services. Sales can be cash sales or credit sales. The difference between cash sales and credit sales is the time you receive payment. If you sell a product and receive payment immediately, it is called cash sales. When you sell on credit, you receive your payment in the future.

The sales account keeps track of all transactions related to sales. At the end of the month or year, the total sales are compared with the sales returns and allowances to get the net sales, which is recorded in the income statement.

Inventory

In financial accounting, goods yet to be sold are referred to as inventory. An organization's inventory refers to goods like raw materials, work-in-progress goods, and finished products that are ready to be sold. As a bookkeeper, you need to record inventory carefully.

Inventory is an asset meant for sale, or a product that is still in the process of production. The inventory account should be created and ensure you record the accurate inventory in this account.

Expenses

No matter how profitable your business is, you will need to spend on some things. You need to spend money to make more money. The salaries, wages, and rents you pay and the machines you repair are all examples of expenses. If you do not spend on labor or you fail to repair that book stapling machine, you cannot generate profit.

Expenses are categorized into two classes: recurring expenses and non-recurring expenses. Recurring expenses are expenses you incur regularly. These expenses are crucial for the smooth running of your business. Examples of recurring expenses are electricity, salaries, rent, travel, and insurance expenses. These expenses are incurred in every accounting period.

Non-recurring expenses are incurred unexpectedly. There are unforeseen expenses that are unlikely to happen during an accounting period. Non-recurring expenses are a one-time expense that is not expected to continue again because they do not occur regularly. Examples include losses incurred due to theft or fire, lawsuit payments, company's write-offs, etc.

Liabilities

Liabilities refer to the debts owed by your business. This involves loans you have gotten from lenders. It also includes payroll expenses and accounts payable. In a liability account, a company records all its obligations, customer deposits, debt, etc. Liabilities refer to the amount you owe your creditors.

You need to keep good records of all liabilities. Examples of liabilities are interest payable, customer deposits, wages payable, income taxes payable, accounts payable, salaries payable, and other accrued expenses.

Account Receivable

If you sell goods or services without collecting payment instantly, it is called receivables. One of the most important accounts you need to keep track of is the account receivable. Ensure you keep your accounts receivable up to date and accurate.

If you want to keep good account receivable balances, you need to create an account receivable report and ensure it is reviewed weekly. The account receivable report contains a list of customer invoices yet to be paid. To keep good records of the amount your customers owe you, you should review the account receivable report regularly.

Owner's Equity

The owner's equity refers to your investment in the business. The owner's equity account keeps records of the amount a business owner invests in the business. It is also known as net assets because it shows the amount of money an owner invested in the business, excluding the liabilities.

In small businesses bookkeeping, the owner's equity account is created to determine the amount of money the business owner invested in the business. You can calculate the owner's equity by summing up the current revenues, owner's capital account, and current contributions and then subtracting expenses and withdrawals.

BOOKKEEPING

CHAPTER 4

ACCOUNTING

Accounting and bookkeeping are related but are different concepts. Many people have studied accounting, and people that studied accounting are called accountants. Accounting is a very important aspect of businesses. Financial accounting helps business owners to determine the financial state of their businesses. This chapter discusses financial accounting and how it can be done in small businesses.

What is Accounting?

Accounting is a broad concept that entails the process of keeping track of financial transactions and summarizing financial transactions. The process of accounting is a vital aspect of businesses that reveals the performance of a business. Evaluating the performance of a business helps a business owner to develop strategies that will lead to a better running of the business.

Even if you do not own a business, accounting is required in our everyday lives. For instance, if you prepare a budget and account for all your expenses and income, then you are making an account of your finances. Small business make use of the accounting process to keep track of their financial details.

Accounting has existed for a long time, and it has helped so many businesses and organizations experience financial growth. Accounting helps you to assess the cash flow, expenses, income, liabilities, and assets of your organization. It is the backbone of a business, and without it, a business will crumble. A business needs financial accounting to thrive.

Accounting derives financial statements from bookkeeping, which helps a business make critical decisions. With the help of accounting, business owners know which strategies were helpful and what to do for the smooth running of their businesses. Accounting is defined as the art of recording, analyzing, measuring, and summarizing financial transactions of an organization.

Importance of Accounting in Small Businesses

Every business spends money and makes sales; accounting makes it easier to track these transactions. Below is the importance of accounting in a business:

Evaluates a Business' Performance

It is important you know the financial performance of your business because you have invested in this business. Accounting gives you a clear picture of what your business is like. Accounting reveals what you need to know about your business. As a business owner, you must know the performance of your business so that you can make good decisions that will improve your business.

The financial statements derived from bookkeeping reflect the financial position of your business. Accounting helps you to know how your business is fairing. As a business owner, it is your responsibility to know the financial health of your business. A business without proper accounting will fail.

Creates Future Projections

The process of accounting helps a business to make plans for the future. When you understand the financial position of your business, you will be able to make budgets and create projections for the future. Sometimes businesses spend on unforeseen projects; making plans for the future can help you solve some financial problems that may arise in the future.

Making future plans and projections for your business is based on past financial data. Business owners compare past and present financial data to make plans for the future. Proper accounting provides accurate and detailed financial statements to help you to create projections and make plans for the future.

Helps You Achieve Your Goal

Proper accounting helps you accomplish your objectives. If your objective is to sell more or acquire more assets, you can achieve this goal by proper accounting. Accounting gives you a clear picture of the financial standing of your business, which will help you plan for the future.

Ensures Statutory Compliance

The law and regulations guiding businesses vary from one state to another. Proper accounting helps you to abide by these laws. For instance, according to the IRS, a business should use the accrual basis of accounting method when they earn over $25 million monthly.

Proper accounting addresses liabilities like VAT, pension funds, income tax, and sales tax properly. Accounting helps your business comply with the laws and regulations related to business in your state.

Basic Accounting Terminology

As a business owner, you should understand some commonly used accounting terms.

Assets

Assets refer to any resources or items owned by your business. Assets often appear on your balance sheet. Examples of assets are inventory, machinery, accounts receivable, a loan given to an employee, etc.

Liabilities

Liabilities refer to the amount owed by a business or organization. Examples of liabilities are tax payable, account payable, equipment loans, etc. Anything your business owes other entities is known as a liability.

Debits

Debits are accounting terms that refer to entries in your ledger. Debits record transactions on the left column of an account. Debits are often balanced by credits when closing your books. Expenses are always debited in the general ledger.

Credits

Credits are the opposite of debits. Credits record transactions at the right column of an account. For each debit entry, there must be a credit entry and vice versa. A credit entry increases an equity account or decreases an expense or asset account.

Income Statement

Income statement states the expense incurred and the income generated from business operations during a financial period. The income statement is a vital financial statement that reveals the financial performance of a business over a given period. It reveals the amount of profit generated in a business or the loss incurred.

The General Ledger

The general ledger records all financial transactions of a business or organization. It consists of the debit and credit column. It records assets, liabilities, income, profits, expenses, and losses.

Expenditure

It is normal for businesses to spend money. Expenditure is anything you spend money on. When your expenditures become greater than your income, then you have incurred a loss. Any cost incurred to get a particular item or to generate revenue is regarded as an expenditure.

Balance Sheet

A balance sheet in financial accounting refers to a financial statement that reports the financial position of a business at a particular time. The balance sheet reports the assets, equity, and liabilities of a business. The balance sheet is one of the most important financial reports in accounting.

Owner's Equity

The owner's equity refers to the amount you own in your business. The owner's equity is the investment of the owner in the business subtracted by the owner's withdrawals from the business with the addition of the net income. As a business owner, you have claims to the equity.

Fixed Costs

Fixed costs are costs that do not change regardless of the business activities. These costs are incurred frequently, and they do not fluctuate with sales. Examples of fixed costs are utility bills, rent, salaries, insurance, property taxes, interest expense, etc. These costs are sometimes called general & administrative or overhead expenses.

Variable Costs

This type of cost is the opposite of fixed costs. These costs change from time to time, based on the financial position of a business. Variable costs are not static; they fluctuate. The level of output in a business or organization determines these costs. Examples of fixed costs include production supply, commissions, freight out, etc.

Capital

Capital in accounting refers to the amount of money or resources used to start up a business. Examples of capital are tangible equipment, buildings, funds in deposit accounts, production equipment, etc. Capital can also be calculated by the deduction of a business liability from its assets.

Return Inwards

Return inwards are goods returned by a customer after they have been sold. Return inwards are recorded in a trading account. Return inwards are always debited in the general ledger.

Return Outwards

Return outwards, also known purchase returns, are goods returned by an organization after they have been purchased. These goods can be returned based on some damage or any other reason.

Branches of Accounting

Accounting is a broad field having several branches. This section explains the different branches of accounting.

Management Accounting

Management accounting is a subfield of accounting that is concerned with financial information that is needed for management. Management accounting utilizes financial data for decision-making purposes. This information is not published; it is used to evaluate the performance of a business, determine the profitability of a business, and to assist in making decisions.

The users of this accounting information are the managers. The accounting information is organized in a way that makes it simple for managers to understand and analyze. This subfield of accounting analyzes financial operations and costs to make financial statements, records, or reports.

Financial Accounting

Financial accounting is one of the branches of accounting that deals with how financial reports are prepared. This branch of accounting involves the interpretation of the financial statements of an organization. It provides users with the necessary financial information. Financial accounting records and summarizes financial transactions of an organization.

Financial accounting abides by the Generally Accepted Accounting Principles. The Generally Accepted Accounting Principles are the rules guiding the preparation of financial reports. They ensure that financial reports are reliable and useful. Several accounting techniques like ledgers, journals, trial balance, etc. are used to keep financial records.

Cost Accounting

Cost accounting is a branch of accounting that records, analyzes, and interprets the cost incurred on a service or product in business. It involves the process of recording, classifying, and determining the costs of goods and services. Cost accounting helps to calculate the cost of every service and product.

Cost accounting involves three major areas: cost reduction, cost control, and cost ascertainment. Cost accounting helps a business to determine the price of a service or product, make better decisions, calculate the break-even point, and prevent wastage. Cost accounting is useful in creating budgets and make plans for an organization.

Auditing

Auditing is a branch of accounting that deals with the examination of the financial statements or reports of an organization to determine its accuracy. Auditing refers to the process of inspecting, reviewing, verifying, and evaluating the financial records of an organization. The person who does this job is regarded as an auditor.

Auditing ensures that the financial records of an organization comply with the rules and regulations guiding accounting. According to accounting laws, all public companies should audit their financial statements. External auditors are not part of the organization's staff; they keep a check on the financial records and provide a statement on these records. Internal auditors are part of the organization; they are employed by the organization to keep a check on financial records.

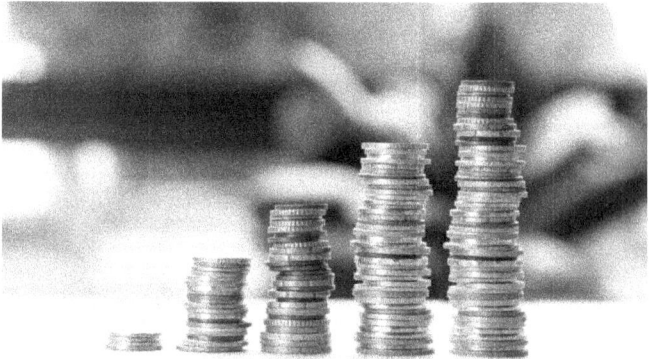

Tax Accounting

Tax accounting is a branch of accounting that is concerned with taxes. The sole purpose of tax accounting is to keep a check on the funds of a company and ensures that a company complies with tax regulations. The rules and regulations guiding tax accounting are the Internal Revenue Code. Businesses and organizations must adhere to the rules and regulations of the IRC when calculating their tax returns.

Tax accounting is concerned with how tax payments and returns are made. The type of tax returns you submit is based on the type of business you operate. A tax accountant can calculate the amount of tax you are required to pay.

There are other branches of accounting, like government accounting, forensic accounting, fund accounting, and fiduciary accounting. All these branches of accounting are concerned with specializing in their field. Accounting is very crucial in businesses, organizations, and the government system.

CHAPTER 5

HOW TO RECORD TRANSACTIONS

Accounting and bookkeeping exist because business transactions exist. Without any business transaction, there is no need for bookkeeping and accounting. Bookkeeping keeps up-to-date and well-detailed records of business transactions. In every organization or business, financial or business transactions exist. This chapter explains what a business transaction is, how to record business transactions, the features of a business transaction, accounting equations, and the classification of a business transaction.

What is a Business Transaction?

Business transaction describes activities and events of a monetary business that has a financial effect on a business. A business transaction is also known as a financial transaction. For instance, you have a business, and you purchase raw materials that are needed for the production of your goods. If you purchase these raw materials and you paid $1000 cash for it, it is a financial activity that affects your business financially.

Bookkeeping and accounting systems only record activities that have a financial impact on the business. The salary you pay to your employees, the goods you purchase, the products you sell to your customers, and the rent you pay are good examples of financial transactions because they all involve money.

Some events do not have a monetary value. These kinds of events cannot be recorded as financial or business transactions. Since business transactions have to deal with money, any other type of event that does not involve money is not regarded as a financial transaction. For example, if a worker volunteers to teach his colleagues some accounting skills without demanding payment, this would not involve a financial transaction. Although this activity has a positive impact on the company, it cannot be classified as a business transaction.

An accountant or a bookkeeper keeps track of the financial transaction by creating a journal entry. The accountant or bookkeeper ensures that business transactions are authorized and supported by some documents before putting it in the journal. Some business transactions are recorded in the sales or purchases journal before posting them to the general ledger, while some transactions are directly recorded in the general ledger.

Features of a Business Transaction

A business transaction is not just recorded; it must have some features that will make it classified and recorded as a business transaction. We need to know that there are financial and non-financial transactions. Therefore, one has to be careful when recording financial transactions. Before you classify and record a transaction as a business transaction, you need to look for the following features or characteristics:

It Must be a Monetary Activity

A transaction that involves money is said to be a business transaction. A business transaction must have a monetary value. For instance, William Productions provides event management services for the sum of $5,000. Such a transaction is a business transaction for William Productions because it involves money.

It Must Involve the Business Entity

A transaction is regarded as a financial if it involves the business entity and affects the business's financial position. If Mr. William, the CEO of William Productions, purchases a car with his own money for his use, such a transaction will not be recorded in the company's account because the transaction does not involve the business.

If Mr. William invests $5,000 into the business, such a transaction will be recorded in the company's account because it involves the business entity and also affects the business's financial position.

It Must have a Dual Impact on the Accounting Elements

A transaction is recorded as a financial transaction when it has a dual effect. This means for each debit entry, there must be a credit entry and vice versa. This is the principle of double-entry accounting.

For instance, William productions bought some drapes for decoration for $3,500. The drapes purchased increased the company's assets. The company gave out some amount of money to get drapes; therefore, there is a decrease in the company's cash. The company's asset account is debited, while the cash account is credited.

It Must have the Support of a Source Document

A financial transaction has to be supported by a source document. A source document contains the original details of a business transaction. A source document records the vital details of a transaction. It makes records of the date, the amount paid, and the names of the entities involved in the transaction.

Source documents are crucial to internal auditors because they are used as a source of evidence. A source document is used as a piece of evidence by a business organization when dealing with their clients. Source documents include checks, invoices, bank statements, sales receipts, payroll reports, and purchase orders.

Classification of Business Transactions

Business transactions are classified into cash and credit transactions and internal and external transactions.

Cash Transaction

A business transaction is classified as a cash transaction if payment is received in cash immediately. In cash transactions, payment can be made with a check or credit card. As long as the payment is made at the time of business transactions, it is a cash transaction.

What differentiates a cash transaction from a credit transaction is the time of payment. Cash sales, purchase of goods by cash, and cash transactions are examples of cash transactions.

Credit Transaction

A credit transaction is a type of transaction in which payment is made at a future date. For instance, if you sell a product to a customer and expect payment at a future date, such a transaction is called a credit transaction.

When credit transaction occurs, the payment is not made at the time the business transactions takes place, which means cash is paid or received at a future time. Most goods are purchased and sold on credit.

Internal Transaction

Internal transactions are transactions made with no external entities involved. It is a transaction in which no outsider is involved. It is a business transaction that is made within the same organization. Provision of services and goods to a department of the same organization and calculating and recording depreciation are good examples of internal transactions.

External Transaction

This refers to a transaction that involves external parties. This kind of transaction occurs between organizations and involves a transaction between a business and another entity. The sale or purchase of goods from another party, purchase of goods from a supplier, and payment of salary are examples of external transactions. The majority of the business transactions recorded are external transactions.

The Rules for Identifying a Cash and Credit Transaction

Sometimes, business owners become confused in determining the type of transaction. There are rules to determine if a transaction is a credit or cash. These rules are explained below.

A transaction is classified as cash if the name of the buyer or seller is not mentioned in the transaction. For instance, purchased goods for $300.

A transaction is recorded as a cash transaction if 'cash' is involved. For example, purchasing goods for $100 from Mr. Edwards.

If "on credit" is mentioned in a transaction, such a transaction is classified as a credit transaction.

If the buyer's or seller's name is mentioned in the transaction. For instance, they purchased goods for $1000 from Mr. Edwards.

All business transactions must have a financial impact on a business. Business transactions affect the asset, owner's equity, revenues, liabilities, and expenses of a business. With these rules, business owners, accountants, and bookkeepers can easily determine if a business transaction is a cash or credit.

Accounting Equations

The accounting equation is the fundamental of accounting and a crucial element of the balance sheet. The accounting equation shows the balance sheet's structure. In the accounting equation, assets are derived by the sum of liabilities and shareholder's equity. Accountants and bookkeepers should always apply the accounting equation when making journal entries.

You can also derive the shareholder's equity by subtracting liabilities from assets, i.e., Shareholder's equity = Assets - Liabilities. The accounting equation must balance. The accounting equation reveals the economic impacts of financial transactions in a business. Liabilities can also be derived by subtracting equity from assets. It reveals how economic activities affect the balance sheet.

The expanded accounting equation reveals the interaction between your balance sheet and income statement. The expanded accounting equation is calculated by Assets = Liabilities + Income + Owner's Equity – Expenses – Draws. Income increases the owner's equity; expenses reduce the owner's equity, and the Owner's draw reduces the owner's equity.

For instance, if Just Rite Enterprise decides to buy a new asset, such as a vehicle that costs $5000, the company can purchase the vehicle by paying with cash (company's assets), with a liability (a loan) or with owner's equity (funds). If the purchase is carried out by using liability, the $ 5,000 can be paid using cash (assets).

The Importance of the Accounting Equation

The accounting equation is very important in accounting and bookkeeping. It shows the interactions that exist among the owner's equity, liabilities, and assets. It is the fundamental of the double-entry system.

Preparation of Financial Reports

The accounting equation is very vital when preparing financial reports. It is used to create a financial report like the balance sheet. The balance sheet is a yearly report that can be prepared quarterly and derived from the accounting equations.

It is the Basis of the Double-Entry System

The accounting equation is the basis of the double-entry system in accounting. It ensures that the books of a company are balanced.

Reveals the Financial Position of a Business

The accounting equation provides the financial performance of your business. If you want to make a financial report of your business, you will need to calculate the accounting equation. The accounting equation reveals the interaction between your income statements and the balance sheet.

Shows the Worth of a Company

Another importance of the accounting equation is that it shows the financial worth of a company. The accounting equation reveals how much your business has in the bank. It helps you to evaluate the value of investments in a business. It helps you to know the net worth of your business. It also helps investors to decide on investing in a company.

Helps to Make Critical Decisions

As a business owner, the accounting equation helps you to make critical decisions in your business. With this equation, you can know if you can go ahead with purchasing an asset or not. It will also reveal if your business is financially capable of paying off debts with the existing assets or by taking more loans.

How Business Transactions are Analyzed

Analysis of business transaction studies how the financial performance of businesses changes due to financial transactions. Different financial transactions affect a business's financial position. Business transactions change the five main elements of accounting, which include capital, income, expenses, assets, and liabilities.

The accounting principle states that every business transaction must have a two-fold effect on a business. For instance, Mrs. Palmer, the CEO of Palmer's Enterprises, buys equipment worth $16,000. This business transaction has a two-fold effect. The equipment, which is the company's asset, will increase by $16,000, and the company's cash, which is also an asset, will decrease by $16,000. Therefore, these changes are reflected in the company's assets.

If the equipment was bought on credit from another organization, there will be two changes. The equipment will increase by $16,000, and the company's liability will increase by $16,000.

How to Record Business Transactions

When analyzing and recording a business transaction, there are certain steps you need to take, these steps are:

Determining the accounts involved: For every business transaction that occurs, there are two or more accounts involved. The first step in analyzing a business transaction is determining the accounts that are involved.

Identifying the nature of the accounts: This is the second procedure you follow when analyzing a business transaction. You need to know if the transaction is an asset account or a capital account.

Determining the impacts based on the decrease and increase: You need to identify the account that is decreasing and the one that is increasing - two accounts can increase at the same time.

Apply the credit and debit rule: This is the last procedure you take when analyzing business transactions. In this procedure, you need to determine the account that needs to be debited and credited.

Journal Entries

A journal is a financial record that keeps track of transactions. Examples of the journal include purchases journal, sales journal, cash disbursements journal, and cash receipts journal. Some transactions are recorded in a journal before they are recorded in the general ledger. The most important journal is the general journal. The general journal records every business transaction carried out in a business.

The sales journal records all sales made on credit or a business's inventory. The return inward journal records goods that were sold but returned by customers. The first place a transaction is recorded in the journal. The general ledger is prepared from the entries made in the journal.

How to Perform Accounting Journal Entries

Before preparing a journal, you need to record the financial details of your transactions. You can get the financial details of your transactions from purchase orders, cash register tapes, invoices, and other sources. Once the transaction has been analyzed, you can record the financial data in the journal. Every transaction recorded in the journal is called a journal entry.

The double-entry system is used when recording transactions in the journal. For every entry, there must be a debit and credit column. For instance, if Mr. A buys machinery with cash, the accounts affected are the asset account and the cash account. The cash account will increase while the asset account will increase.

The single-entry system can also be used for recording transactions in the journal, but this system is rarely used. In this system, only a single account exists for every entry made in the journal. While balancing the journal, make sure the credits and the debit balance well.

The Difference Between a General Ledger a Journal

Financial transactions are recorded in the general ledger and journal. The journal is a document where transactions are recorded first before they are entered in the ledger. The general ledger summarizes financial information.

The journal keeps a record of all financial transactions carried out in business while the ledger records the financial details used for preparing financial statements. The journal, which is always referred to as a document of original entry, is used for making ledger while the ledger is used for preparing final accounts and trial balance.

Entries recorded in the journal are done in chronological order, while transactions are posted in the general ledger by using the double-entry system. You do not need to balance the journal, but the general ledger needs to be balanced.

Bookkeepers and accountants make use of the general ledger to keep track of all relevant accounts. The general ledger has the debit and the credit side, and it uses the T format when recording transactions.

Debits/Credits

In the accounting world, the debit side is the left side of an account, while the credit side is the right side of an account. For every business transaction, there must be credit as well as a debit entry. The principle of double-entry reveals that for each debit entry, a credit entry must be available and vice versa.

When recording a business transaction, you need to determine the two accounts involved. After you have done that, you need to know the accounts that will be debited and the one to be credited. Your journal entries are prepared so that the debit side is at the left and credit side on the right.

In the journal entry, the debit side records an increase in assets and any decrease in the owner's equity and liabilities. For example, if a company purchases a vehicle, the company's assets account will be debited while the cash account is credited since the company's cash is decreasing.

The debit total and the credit total must balance according to the principles of the double-entry system. When the two entries are well balanced, it shows that there are no errors in the transactions recorded. For instance, if a company purchases office supplies with $200 cash, there are two accounts involved, the cash account and the office supplies account. $200 is credited in the cash account, while $500 is debited in the office supplies account.

Let us take a look at the following examples:

Step 1

If Mr. Andrews uses $300,000 to start his business.

Transaction analysis:

Two changes have occurred because of this financial transaction;

1. The owner's equity has increased by $300,000.

2. Cash (an asset) has increased by $300,000.

Step 2

If he deposits $80,000 in the bank

Transaction Analysis:

This transaction has resulted in two changes

1. The cash balance (an asset) will decrease by $80,000

2. The bank balance (an asset) will increase by $80,000

Step 3

If he takes a loan of $50,000 from Mr. Whitney at 10% per annum.

Transaction Analysis:

1. The cash balance increases by $50,000.

2. The liability increases by $50,000.

Step 4

If he buys furniture for $50,000 by cash.

Transaction Analysis:

The two changes that occurred due to this transaction are:

1. The asset has increased by $50,000

2. The cash balance has decreased by $50,000

Step 5

If he buys goods from Mr. Walker for $70,000 and paid with cash $50,000

Transaction analysis:

Three changes have occurred due to this transaction; they are:

1. Purchases (goods) have increased by $70,000

2. Cash balance has decreased by $50,000

3. Liability has increased by $20,000

BOOKKEEPING

CHAPTER 6

ESTABLISHING A SYSTEM

In the old days, business owners, accountants, and bookkeepers recorded transactions using the paper process. They used paper and pencil to make lots of columns, record transactions, and prepare financial statements. In today's world, the story has taken another dimension because several accounting applications have been developed to record transactions.

Business owners can decide to perform the bookkeeping or accounting tasks themselves. Some accounting software can be used to record transactions and perform bookkeeping tasks. Even small business owners can find suitable accounting software for their businesses. There are lots of benefits business owners get from using accounting software.

This chapter discusses the functions and benefits of accounting software, the types of accounting software, how to choose the right accounting software for your business, and how much it costs to get accounting software.

Excel – Spreadsheets

The Microsoft Excel spreadsheet is one of the applications designed to perform accounting tasks. Excel helps to perform tasks like preparation of financial statements, preparation of balance sheets, performing some calculations, etc. Excel spreadsheets can be used to keep track of business transactions. With these spreadsheets, accountants can prepare some accounts which can be stored in the computer and used for decision making.

Excel spreadsheets are commonly used by accountants. These spreadsheets help users organize and summarize data in an easy to use format. Regardless of the size of your business, Microsoft Excel spreadsheets can be used to perform accounting tasks. As a small business owner, Excel helps you to tabulate, organize, calculate, summarize, and store accounting data.

In Excel, you can use the cash basis or the accrual basis method of accounting. When using the accrual method, you have to set up different accounts. When adopting the double-entry principle, you have to make use of the accounting equation.

If you prefer the cash basis method, you need to prepare a new worksheet and put column headers for the transaction description, date, and transaction number. Accountants have long used Microsoft Excel, and it has proved to be a useful and reliable application.

Accounting Software - QuickBooks

What is Accounting Software?

Accounting software is an application used by accountants to keep track of the flow of cash for external and internal review. It is a financial tool that helps a business to evaluate its financial performance. Accounting software abides by the laws guiding accounting. Accounting software helps to reduce mistakes that can be made using a pencil and paper.

Accounting software helps you to get sales projections for the next quarter, evaluate the financial performance of your business, and determine the items you need in your business. Accounting software offers a wide variety of benefits for users. If you want to run a successful business, you need to consider using effective accounting software.

Accounting software should abide by the accounting rules and regulations of your state or country. For instance, if you are in the United Kingdom, the choice of your accounting software should comply with Making

Tax Digital. In the United States, accounting software should comply with the Sweeping Tax Cuts and Jobs Act.

Examples of Accounting Software

FreeAgent

FreeAgent is an accounting software that helps bookkeepers, accountants, and business owners to manage their transactions. This software carries out the management of invoices, payroll, expenses, and other accounting activities. FreeAgent makes use of the double-entry method of accounting, which makes it user-friendly.

FreshBooks

FreshBooks is an effective accounting applications you can use to perform your accounting and bookkeeping tasks. Over 5 million organizations around the globe use this software. This software is suitable for small businesses that want to operate following the regulations and standards of their state or country. FreshBooks is a mobile-friendly software that is very easy to operate.

Zoho Books

Zoho Books is a powerful online software that offers a wide variety of features that help small businesses to manage cash flow in their business. Purchase and sale order management, management of expenditure, invoicing, time tracking, contact management, and inventory management are some of the features offered by this accounting software.

Zoho Books is a high-quality application that automates payment reminders, bank statements, and invoices. It provides upgrades on some of its features, such as custom domains and invoice templates.

Tipalti

This accounting software is created to make the process of account payable easier. Some features it offers include automation of invoice, calculation of tax, regulatory compliance management, supplier management, and payment remittance. Tipalti ensures that the financial data of your business is processed in an easy to understand language.

With this software, issues like non-compliance, late payments, and over-tasking the accountant are prevented. Tipalti features ERP systems, payment reconciliation, and AP. This software makes global mass payments very simple. With Tipalti, you can make use of 120 currency options and depend on six different methods of payment like debit card, PayPal, local bank transfer, and wire.

Sage Business Cloud Accounting

For small business owners that need effective accounting software, Sage business cloud accounting has got you covered. It provides features that meet the requirement of small business accounting. For small business owners, you can utilize the entry-level accounting solution with Sage.

It provides features like minimizing spreadsheets, managing finances, and reducing paperwork. This software makes business payroll simple and easy to handle, manages cash flow, and automates financial processes.

Tradogram

This software is specifically developed to ensure the smooth running of the purchasing process of your business. The software features built-in tools that help in tracking expenses, managing suppliers, and controlling costs. Tradogram offers some accounting tools for generating contracts, invoices, Pos, and other documents.

Xero

Xero helps small business owners and financial managers to have access to financial information on any device. This application is mobile-friendly. It helps small business owners to keep track of account receivables, expenditures, account payables, revenues, and wages. With Xero, you can reconcile your bank transactions.

Types of Accounting Software

There are different kinds of accounting software you can use for your small business. When choosing accounting software, it should be based on the type and nature of your business. There are four major categories of accounting software. The four categories are:

Payroll Management Systems

If you want to take charge of your account receivables and account payables, you should consider opting for the payroll management system. These applications were designed to carry out different business tasks, such as employees' salaries calculation, pay slips and tax forms, cutting deductions, etc. This category of accounting software will keep your financial transactions secure and help you make detailed financial reports. Examples of payroll management systems include AccountEdge, Xero, and Zenefits.

Time and Expense Management Systems

Applications that belong to this category include Zoho Expense, FreshBooks, and Expensify. These applications are specifically developed to speed up billing cycles. They make the payment process faster and help detect slow and inefficient payment processes. The greatest benefit these systems offer is the production of detailed graphs on how resources and time can be managed within a company.

Billing and Invoicing Systems

Zoho Books, FreshBooks, and Zoho Invoice are examples of applications that belong to this category. These applications help businesses to complete basic and daily tasks. These tasks include informing clients about due payments and check writing. These systems feature invoicing and billing tools that help to prepare a financial event for validation and authorization.

Enterprise Resource Planning Systems

This category of accounting software is important. It includes the systems required for inventory management, cost control, finance, material purchasing, human resource, finance, product planning, and accounting. Newly designed ERP solutions provide modules for Customer relations Management and business intelligence. Applications like Odoo, Intact, and Brightpearl belong to this category.

Functions of Accounting Software

Billing and invoicing: Some accounting applications are specifically designed for carrying out the tasks of invoicing and billing. When you need to know who owes you money, the amount, and the due date for payment, accounting software has got you covered. Most accounting systems enable you to print invoices and send them to your customers through email. Your accounting system will provide information as regards the name, account numbers, and address of the customer.

These accounting systems also provide automatic invoicing. Automatic invoicing in accounting systems ensure that your income is not delayed, even if you have forgotten to send an invoice. The accounting software reminds your customers when to pay their bills.

Payroll management: Accounting software offers a wide variety of payroll features that will help you to calculate the employee payments and also print checks quickly. In some accounting systems, payroll modules are very effective. They are in control of all aspects of payroll.

Accounting software helps to handle various pay schedules having various kinds of compensation in your company. Some workers are paid daily, weekly, or monthly; the accounting software will help you to handle these payments.

Forecasting and budgeting: Accounting software helps businesses to plan and make a budget. Most accounting applications provide details about the financial performance of a business by calculating and interpreting the company's financial data. With effective accounting software, small businesses and companies can make a budget for the future.

With the provision of necessary financial details, companies can make critical decisions as regards their finances. Businesses can also make feasible goals.

Accounting: Accounting software performs accounting tasks. An effective accounting system should consist of features like accounts payable, account receivables, general ledgers, etc. The primary component of every accounting system is accounting.

Inventory management: An accounting application that features inventory and stock controls can help you to know what you have in stock and what you need to purchase. Accounting software helps you track and manage your inventory, know the type of stocks you need to get and determine stock locations.

Banking: Accounting software helps you to make payments directly from your bank and as well enable you to import information directly from the bank into the accounting system. If your business uses more than one bank account, you should get an accounting system that will help you reconcile your accounts.

Accounting software also helps you to make payments with the use of checks. Some systems offer features that enable you to process and print your checks. They also provide features like bank deposits preparation, check to handle, and check to void.

Time management: This is an important function performed by accounting systems. Most businesses and companies need to track the time spent on accomplishing specific tasks. Time modules offered by accounting systems are very helpful in tracking the time an employee spent in accomplishing a task. This ensures you calculate the accurate payroll in your business.

Shipping: Some accounting systems save you the stress and money to invest in shipment software. As a business owner that often sends goods using a courier service, you can consider opting for accounting systems that make the process of shipping goods easier.

With this accounting system, you can easily track what you have shipped and calculate delivery times accurately. Some applications help you to know how distance and weight vary; this will help you calculate accurate shipping costs.

Why You Should Use Accounting Software

There are several benefits you enjoy when you use accounting software. Accounting software is a tool used by most accountants and bookkeepers to perform accounting and bookkeeping tasks. These applications can make the tax returns calculation easy and also comply with specific requirements in your state or country. You should use accounting software for the following reasons:

It is easy to use: It provides information that can be understood by an audience who has little or no experience in accounting. With accounting software, a business owner can perform all accounting tasks without hiring an external party to perform the tasks.

It saves money: With effective accounting software, you do not need to hire an external expert to help you perform your accounting tasks. Accounting software helps you perform calculations and administrative tasks and as well manage your revenue. Accounting applications reduce the cost of printing documents.

It complies with tax rules: This is one of the benefits of using accounting software. Most accounting applications abide by tax rules and regulations. Immediately they are installed; they carry out their accounting tasks with compliance to the tax rules.

It helps to improve performance: If a business owner needs to improve the performance of her business, she should consider using accounting software. Accounting software collects, organizes, and summarizes the crucial part of the accounting data available. With the information provided by accounting software, you can evaluate your business's performance and make decisions that will improve your business.

It provides security: A company's financial data is vital information that needs to be kept securely. This data should not fall into the wrong hands. Accounting software ensures the security of your financial data. In most cases, they always come with a password.

It is transparent: Accounting applications provide automating calculations. One of the benefits of using accounting software is that it prevents costly errors. Previously, lots of errors were made when using the paper and pencil method. Errors can mislead a business and negatively affect business performance.

Factors to Consider When Choosing Accounting Software for Your Small Business

Accounting software offers lots of benefits for users. It is easier, faster, more efficient, and better than the pencil and paper method. As a small business owner, your top priority is the financial performance of your business and how to improve it.

You need an accounting system that will help you perform and accomplish your accounting tasks as well as give you a clear picture of the financial performance of your business. One of the most critical decisions you will make as a business owner is choosing the right accounting software for your business. Each software offers different features and several pricing plans you can opt for. You need to consider some factors before choosing an accounting system; these factors are discussed below:

Ease of use: You need to consider how easy and simple the accounting software you are opting for is. The information should be well-arranged, and calculations should be made simple.

Mobile-ready: This is an important factor you should take into consideration. These days, most accounting systems offer iOS and Android applications for users. The mobile apps also offer the same features as the desktop versions.

Cost: The price of accounting software varies; this depends on the number of features and the kinds of plans it offers. Some companies provide users with a free version of their accounting applications. You should opt for an accounting system that meets your budget.

Security: Accounting software keeps the vital information of a business; therefore, you need to consider the security mechanism of your preferred software.

Multi-user support: You need accounting software that will support several small businesses with one account. This should be an important factor for business owners with multiple businesses. If your software features multi-user support, it saves you the cost of establishing separate accounts for every entity.

CHAPTER 7

GENERAL LEDGER

The Charts of Accounts, general ledger, and Journal are vital accounts in bookkeeping. In the double-entry bookkeeping system, business transactions are recorded in the journal and general ledger. This chapter explains the general ledger, journal, and trial balance. It discusses how transactions are recorded in these three books.

General Ledger: What Does This Mean?

The general ledger is an important book in accounting that utilizes the double-entry system. In the traditional sense, accountants and bookkeepers record business transactions in the general ledger by utilizing the double-entry system of accounting. The advancement in technology has made the preparation of ledger easier. There are excel sheets and accounting software that can help you prepare ledgers.

Most financial reports are derived from the ledger. The general ledger records and summarizes all the business transactions that occur in an organization. This accounting document ensures that all entries have a debit and credit record. An entry in an account must have an opposite entry in another. The general ledger operates per the double-entry principle, which states that "for each credit entry, there must be a debit entry and vice versa."

Why a General Ledger is Important

The general ledger is very important in accounting. Small business owners can prepare the general ledger to record financial transactions carried out in their businesses. Although the general ledger is not compulsory, you can decide not to use it based on the nature of your business. The general ledger is important because it does the following:

- It gives a clear picture of your business at any time. For instance, a cash ledger will show the cash in hand at a particular time.

- It makes the process of bank reconciliation faster because all financial transactions related to a bank account are recorded in one place.

- It gives reports of expenses and revenues which help you know what to spend on.

- Auditors require it because it reflects the transactions carried out in your business.

- It helps you to detect any fraudulent practices in your business.

- With the general ledger, filing tax returns is easier since all your revenue and expenses are recorded in one place.

Posting Transactions to Separate Ledger Account

A general ledger contains separate accounts like purchases, cash, sales, etc. Journal entries are posted in the ledger account. When posting entries in the general ledger, you need to open a separate account for every account, and transactions from the journal are transferred to each ledger account.

If you debit any account in the journal, you will also debit it in the ledger account. All transactions in the journal entry must be recorded in the ledger account. As a business owner, you need to post your transactions in the general ledger.

For instance, if a company sold goods worth $3,000 for cash, there are two separate accounts in this business transaction. The separate accounts opened in the general ledger are cash account and sales account. The cash account is debited, while the sales account is credited

The cash account is receiving some cash, while the sales account will decrease by $3,000.

The general ledger includes accounts like cash, accounts payable, capital stock, notes payable, office equipment, etc. Entries in the journal are recorded in the general ledger using the double-entry system. The ledger accounts records transactions associated with a particular account. For instance, sales are recorded in the sales account, purchases are recorded in the purchases account, and account receivable is recorded in the account receivable account, and so on.

The Charts of Account

The Charts of Accounts keeps all the accounts prepared for recording a financial transaction. It is a document that lists all the accounts required in the general ledger of a business. Several business transactions are carried out daily in a company. A Chart of Accounts consists of equity, assets, income, expenditure, and liabilities.

The Chart of Accounts provides all the business transactions carried out in a company during an accounting period. It describes the name of every account that is listed and the identification number of each account. The chart of accounts includes the income statement accounts and balance sheet accounts.

The Chart of Accounts is a vital financial aspect of a business because it is specifically designed to record all the liability, revenue, assets, equity, and expenses of the organization. A company can design its chart of accounts based on the type of business it is operating. Chart of accounts is a useful source of financial information for external parties that need to know about an organization.

The chart of account provides the necessary information about a company and its daily operations. A small business needs to set up its CoA when starting a business. The chart of accounts is set up based on the nature or type of business operated.

How to Set Up the Chart of Accounts

A Chart of Accounts is created based on the nature of the business. For instance, business rendering catering services will create certain accounts that are related to the catering business. The catering business can include a transport expense account, which might not be common in all businesses. This catering business might exclude the inventory account since the business renders services.

Identification codes are included in the CoA, and these codes help you to identify some accounts easily. Identification codes enable you to record transactions easily. A three-digit number is often used in small businesses, while a four-digit number is often used in larger businesses. You need to ensure that the numbering follows a pattern to make work easier for the management.

The number of accounts in the CoA depends on the size of the organization - larger businesses with several divisions will typically have more accounts than the smaller businesses. The Chart of Accounts must be prepared according to the Financial Accounting Standards Board and Generally Accepted Accounting Principles.

The Categories of Chart of Accounts

The Chart of Account is categorized into two financial statements - the balance sheet and the income statement.

Balance Sheet Accounts

The balance sheet is a financial statement that consists of liability accounts, asset accounts, and the owner's equity account.

Asset accounts

The asset account contains the records of a company's assets. Assets are classified as current assets and fixed assets, tangible or intangible assets. Examples of a company's assets are cash in hand, inventory assets, savings account, and prepaid insurance.

Liability accounts

The liability account is the record of the debts owed by a company. Examples of liabilities include invoice payable, salary payable, account payable, etc. Just like the asset account, in the liability accounts, current liabilities come before long-term liabilities.

Owner's equity accounts

The owner's equity account reflects the net worth of business after liabilities have been subtracted from the company's assets. The owner's equity reveals the net worth of businesses to shareholders. Examples of transactions recorded in this account include retained profits, common stock, and preferred stocks.

The Income Statement

The income statement is one of the most important financial reports of a company. This statement reflects the profit generated and the loss incurred in a business during an accounting period. The statement records all income and subtracts all expenses from the income. By doing this, the profit or loss of a company is determined. The purpose of this statement is to quickly show investors whether the business made money or lost money.

The Importance of the Chart of Accounts

- It keeps records of all business transactions.

- It reflects the financial position of a business and provides a clear picture of your business.

- It can be designed based on the nature of the business

- It helps to prepare the financial reports of a company.

- It is easy to control costs because it records all accounts separately.

- It helps your business adhere to financial reporting principles.

The Chart of Accounts, journal, and general ledger are very vital in accounting. Small business owners should use these accounts when recording transactions as they provide lots of benefits for business owners. If you want to run a successful business, you should consider using these financial documents since they reflect the financial position of a business.

BOOKKEEPING

CHAPTER 8

PREPARING TRIAL BALANCE FOR SMALL BUSINESSES

After the general ledger has been prepared, you must prepare a trial balance for your small business. This chapter discusses the usefulness of trial balance and how you can prepare a trial balance for your small business.

As a small business owner, you may not like performing bookkeeping and accounting tasks, but you need to perform these tasks to run a successful business. You need to prepare the trial balance to ensure that your accounts are correctly recorded. The trial balance will help you detect some mistakes in your double-entry books.

The Meaning of a Trial Balance

A trial balance is a financial report in which the balances of the general ledger of a business are recorded at a particular point in time. The accounts recorded in trial balance are associated with the major accounting items such as liabilities, income, expenses, assets, equity, profit, and loss. The trial balance is used to determine the balance of credit and debit entries from the general ledger at a particular period.

The trial balance helps to adjust some entries in the general ledger. It is prepared to ensure that the total credits and debits are well balanced. The trial balance is not officially or legally required from businesses. It is only prepared for people within an organization and not be distributed to external parties.

The trial balance contains the entire accounts' total in the general ledger. Every account should have a description of the account, an account number, and its final credit or debit balance. Furthermore, the final date of the period the report is prepared should be included in the trial balance.

The primary difference between the general ledger and the trial balance is that the trial balance records the account totals from the general ledger, while the general ledger records all the transactions separately by account.

If any adjustments are to be made, it must show on a trial balance.

Errors That Can't Be Detected in a Trial Balance

Although a trial balance can reveal some inaccuracies of the general ledger, there are some errors this financial report cannot detect. These errors include:

An error of original entry: This occurs when the wrong amount is recorded on the debit and credit side.

An error of omission: This type of error occurs when the transaction is not recorded in the system.

Reversal error: This happens when a transaction is recorded with the correct amount, but the account meant to be credited is debited, while the one to be debited is credited.

Principle error: Principle error occurs when the transaction entered goes against the principles of accounting. For instance, the right amount is entered at the appropriate place, but the type of account the transaction recorded is wrong, e.g., using the asset account instead of the expense account.

Commission error: Commission error occurs when the amount of transaction is right, but the wrong account is credited or debited. Although commission errors may look like the error of principle, commission error occurs due to oversight and not a lack of knowledge.

How to Prepare a Trial Balance

Preparing a trial balance can be a challenging task for small business owners that already have the responsibility of recording their profits and losses, filing taxes returns, issuing invoices, and paying bills. Nevertheless, a trial balance is important for small businesses as it summarizes all the accounts of the general ledger and as well as detects errors in the ledger.

These days, technology advancements have made most accounting and bookkeeping tasks easier and faster to do. Accounting software can help you to prepare your trial balance; this accounting software helps you to remove errors made in the trial balance. The trial balance remains to be an important and useful financial document to businesses.

When preparing a trial balance, your general ledger is used to get the necessary information. The first step is that you separate credits from debits by accounts. A typical trial balance includes three columns: the accounts, debit side, and credit side. The debit side, which is on the left, can be represented with (DR) while the credit side (CR).

A trial balance uses the T-account. After setting up your format, then you will check the entries in the general ledger. You will enter the details from your general ledger into your trial balance. You need to list the name of the account and the amount of each account in the trial balance.

After doing this, you are required to add all the amounts on the debit side to derive the total debits. You can also adopt the same method to derive the total credit. If the credit total and the debit total are equal, your trial balance is well balanced. If the two totals do not match, your trial balance is unbalanced. According to the double-entry principle, your credit total must balance with your debit total.

If your trial balance is not balanced, you have to look for the reasons behind it. Once you detect the errors, you can then make necessary adjustments. You can detect errors by checking all the accounts included in your general ledger. The trial balance is as easy as that.

What a Working Trial Balance Is

Sometimes, a trial balance needs to be adjusted due to errors. When a business has a working trial balance, it refers to the account that is still worked on while making certain adjustments. The trial balance is referred to as a work-in-progress at that particular time. When the work-in-progress is accomplished, the result is referred to as an adjusted trial balance.

The adjusted trial balance is a balance sheet that has been updated after making some necessary adjustments to the account totals. Accountants prepare financial statements by utilizing the information on the adjusted trial balance.

To prepare a financial statement that is free from error, the first step is preparing a trial balance sheet and ensure that the credit and debit entries are equal. The trial balance is majorly prepared by business owners to reflect inaccuracies in financial records. When these errors are detected, the trial balance should be adjusted.

The T-account is used in preparing the trial balance, and it has the debit and credit sides. A working trial balance is a financial record in which adjustments are still being made.

Post-Closing Trial Balance

This is the last procedure in the preparation of a trial balance. The difference between post-closing trial balance and other trial balances is that the balance in the expense and income accounts must be zero. To decide the amount of income and expenses for a given period, one needs to begin with a Zero balance in the expense and income accounts.

With the post-closing trial balance, you can confirm if the balances of these accounts are zero. It also helps you to know if the debit amounts match with the credit amounts after you have closed the entries.

The Importance of a Trial Balance in Small Businesses

The importance of a trial balance cannot be underestimated. It is an important report for small businesses. As a business owner, anytime you prepare your general ledger, you need to check its accuracy. The trial balance helps you to accomplish this by:

Verifying the accuracy of your calculations

The trial balance helps you to check the accuracy of the general ledger. It ensures that the exact amount is recorded in the correct side, while posting the account's total from the different ledger books.

Helping you to prepare financial statements

The accounts in the ledger that are posted in the trial balance are further used for the preparation of financial statements, such as cash flow statement, income statement, and balance sheet. Therefore, the trial balance makes the preparation and analysis of these financial statements easier.

Helping your business to make a comparative analysis

With the trial balance in a business, a business can easily make a comparison between the current and past year balances. Such practices will enable a business to decide on its expenses, income, liabilities, and production costs. You can also take critical actions as long as you already have a clear picture of the present and past trends.

Detecting and correcting errors

In trial balance, the two totals of the two sides must be equal, i.e., the total on the debit side must be the same as the total on the credit side. If the two sides are not balanced, it reflects an inaccuracy. Accountants can detect and correct these errors.

Helping you to make adjustments

When preparing the trial balance, accounts such as outstanding liabilities, closing stock, prepaid expenses must be prepared. Doing this helps you to make the necessary adjustments in the current accounting year. At the end of each accounting year, businesses set up adjustment accounts.

Preparing an effective budget

The trial balance helps businesses make a comparison between the present and past ledger accounts. It also helps business owners follow or adjust the trend of their businesses' performance. After analyzing the performance of your business, you can then make budgets that will have a positive impact on your business.

Preparing audit reports

One of the financial experts that make use of the trial balance is the auditor. With the trial balance, auditors can easily identify the entries in the ledger. The trial balance provides an audit trail that is needed by auditors.

The trial balance summarizes all accounts in the ledger at the end of each accounting period. The trial balance is used for the preparation of trading profit and loss account and balance sheet.

The Difference Between the Trial Balance and Balance Sheet

- The trial balance verifies the accuracy of the calculations of the books of calculation, while the balance sheet reveals the exact financial position of a business.

- The trial balance is derived from the balances of all the accounts in the ledger, while the balance sheet contains the liabilities and assets accounts.

- Accountants prepare the trial balance before preparing the final accounts, while the balance sheet is prepared after the trading, profit and loss account has been prepared.

- The trial balance is used internally, while the balance sheet is used by external parties such as creditors, investors, etc.

- Trial balances can be prepared several times in an accounting period while balance sheets are prepared at the end of an accounting year.

CHAPTER 9

THE CASH BOOK AND CASH FLOW STATEMENT

All businesses make cash transactions. Cash is classified as a current asset of a business, used as a medium of exchange. Business transactions can be carried out by cash or on credit.

Currency notes and coins are examples of cash in accounting. The cash balance in a business is very important. This chapter explains how a cash book is prepared, the significance of a cash book in small businesses, and the types of cash books.

What is a Cash Book?

A cash book is a financial document that is used for recording payments made by cash. It is an essential account that records every cash transaction of business. It performs the function of a general ledger and a journal. The transactions related to cash payment and receipt are recorded in the cash book and then entered in the general ledger.

To have a better understanding of what the cash book does, we can explain the meaning of the two words, cash and book. Cash refers to an item that has monetary value like currency, coins, and checks. These items are used to pay for goods and services. In accounting, a book means a record of financial details that is in written form.

Therefore, the cash book records all financial transactions carried out with cash in a given period. The cash book records transactions carried out thorough checks and discounts given or received based on the type of cash book you prepare. The cash book is very useful for making accounting reports, tracking the flow of cash, and preparing taxes.

The Features of a Cash Book

To understand what a cash book is, one needs to know the features of a cash book. The features include:

- Dual entry: Like other accounting documents, a cash book has credit and debit entries. The debit entry reflects all increases in cash, while the credit entry reflects all transactions that lead to a decrease in cash.

- Performs the function of a journal and ledger: A cash book carries out the function of a general ledger and a journal.

- It must have a debit balance: The cash book records payments made by cash. Cash on hand helps to meet daily expenses in a business. Therefore, it is not possible to pay more than the cash in hand. As a result of this, the business will have a debit cash balance or no cash balance.

- Two equal sides: in accounting, the total of the debit entries of the cash book must be equal with the credit entries.

- Verifiable: The cash balance at the debit side can be re-checked by summing the cash in hand in the business.

Types of Cash Books

A cash book is designed based on the nature of a business and its requirements. A cashbook can be classified into two categories: general cash book and petty cash book.

General Cash Book

The general cash book first records cash transactions in a business and replace the ledger's cash account. The general cash book is divided into three classes.

Single Column Cash Book

The single-column cash book keeps track of all cash transactions. Cash payments are entered in the right column, while receipts will be recorded on the left column. This type of cash book does not keep track of bank transactions, discounts received, or discounts given.

Bank transactions and discounts are recorded in separate ledger accounts. Some businesses use a single column cash book. Cash books always have a debit balance and do not have a credit balance.

Double Column Cash Book

The double-column cash book keeps track of two kinds of transactions in two separate columns. There are two columns in this cash book. It records both cash transactions and discounts. Therefore, the discount given and received can be recorded in this cash book.

A discount is classified as a nominal account. Therefore, the discount received is regarded as a profit and is recorded on the credit side, while discounts given are recorded on the debit side because it is considered a loss.

Three Column Cash Book

The three-column cash book keeps track of cash, discount, and bank transactions. Most organizations use checks as a means of payment these days; therefore, a bank column included in your cash book makes work easier for you. The three-column cash book has a separate column where bank transactions are recorded.

If you received payment by check and the money is deposited the same day, the transaction is recorded on the debit side of the bank column. If the check was sent a day after the payment was received, it is recorded as a contra entry. A contra entry refers to the business transactions that occur between a bank account and a cash account.

Petty Cash Book

A petty cash book records several small cash transactions. Some transactions occur frequently, and these transactions are a small amount of money; therefore, the petty cash book keeps a record of such transactions. The person who manages a petty cash book is called a petty cashier.

Examples of transactions recorded in the petty cash book include food bills, postage, fuel expenses, stationery, cleaning, traveling, newspapers, office teas, etc. Petty transactions are often paid for using currency notes or coins. This type of cash book only records small transactions that are frequently made.

The petty cash book features a credit and debit side. Any payment is entered on the credit side, while receipts are entered on the debit side. In the general cash book, payment made for petty expenses are recorded on the credit side, but this is different in the petty cash book. Payment made for petty expenses are recorded on the petty cash book's debit side.

Elements of a Cash Book

You can understand a cash book by knowing its elements. The cash book has some elements that are explained below.

Date: In the cash book, the date of every transaction that occurs is recorded in the date column. The year is written on the top of the column.

Particulars: The particulars column of a cash book mentions the second account that is involved in a business transaction apart from cash. If the account is described with 'By,' the account is debited; it is credited if described with 'To.'

Voucher Number: If a business receives payment from a customer by cash, the business will give a receipt voucher. The number on the receipt voucher is recorded in front of the transaction made. When the business also makes a payment for any transaction, the business also receives a payment voucher. Receipt and payment vouchers are recorded in the Voucher Number Column.

Amount: The amount of the transaction made is recorded in two columns. In the cash book, the debit column records cash received, and the credit column records cash payments.

Bank: The bank column records all payments received or made by checks. Other types of bank transactions are also recorded in the bank column. The double-column cash book and three column cash book records bank transactions.

Discount: The discount column keeps records of discounts received and discounts allowed. Discount received is a discount given to a business when making purchases, while a discount allowed is a discount given to customers for the sale of a product. The discount allowed is recorded on the credit side of the discount column, while the discount received is recorded at the debit side of the discount column.

The Benefits of Cash Book

The cash book is very important in accounting and offers several benefits for business owners. Large and small business owners can use it. The type of cash book adopted depends on the type of business you operate.

If your business is a small one and you do not use checks or any other bank transactions, you can use the single column cash book. For large business owners that deal with bank transactions and also give and receive discounts, the three-column cash book or the two-column cash book can be used. The benefits of the cash book are discussed below.

- Keeps track of cash transactions: The cash book is a useful book of account that records all cash transactions in an organization.

- Determines cash present at hand: It helps you to know the amount of cash available in the organization.

- Records payments and receipts: This is another benefit of the cash book. With the cash book, you can determine cash payments made and cash receipts given at a particular date.

- Detects errors: With the cash book, you can easily detect errors by verifying the cash book balance. To verify the cash book, you can match the cash book balance with the exact cash in hand.

- Detects fraud: The cash book helps you detect theft or fraudulent practices carried out in your organization.

The Cash Flow Statement

The cash flow statement refers to a financial report that states the amount of cash earned and spent in a company. It reveals how cash is moving into and moving out of a business organization. It is also called the statement of cash flow; it is one of the primary financial statements used by financial analysts.

The cash flow statement reflects and evaluates how an organization manages its cash. It reveals how the performance of the balance sheet accounts and income statements influence the flow of cash. Accountants, shareholders, potential investors, analysts, employees, creditors, and contractors are the people interested in the statement of cash flow of an organization.

This financial statement is specifically designed to offer the necessary information on a business's solvency and liquidity. The cash flow statement is primarily concerned about how cash is generated and spent.

The Main Components of the Cash Flow Statement

The cash flow statement is divided into three major components, which are:

- The flow of cash from operating activities

- The flow of cash from investment

- The flow of cash from financing activities

The cash flow statement sometimes adds a disclosure of non-cash activities as part of the components according to the Generally Accepted Accounting Principles. The cash flow statement is different from the balance sheet account and the income statement.

Cash Flow from Operating Activities

Operating activities involve the manufacturing of goods, sales of goods, receiving payments from customers, and delivering the products of a company. These are activities that generate revenue for a business. These activities have to deal with purchases, sales, and expenses that will generate revenue for the business.

These expenses can be advertising, shipping the goods, purchasing raw materials, and building inventory. Cash flow from operating activities is the cash generated from the income of a company; it excludes costs related to investment in securities or investment on capital items.

The flow of cash from operating activities can be derived by using the direct and indirect method. The direct method reflects how the in-flow and out-flow of cash in the business affect all liability and current asset account. The indirect method reflects how profit is reconciled with cash flow.

Cash Flow from Investing Activities

Investing activities include loans given to suppliers, the sales of assets, purchases of assets, payments linked to acquisitions and mergers, and dividends received from another organization. Cash flow from investment refers to activities that are linked to the sale or purchase of capital assets.

Investing activities refer to activities that generate gain over a long-term period. They lead to changes in non-current assets like equipment, government bonds, investment in shares, etc. Investing activities have nothing to do with cash from external investors like shareholders or bondholders.

For instance, if a company pays out a dividend to its investors, this type of activity is not an investing activity; it is called a financing activity. Examples of investment activities include cash generated from selling an asset, cash spent on the purchase of an asset, cash generated as a result of the merger, cash generated from another company's acquisition.

Cash Flow from Financing Activities

Financing activities refer to events that lead to changes in the composition and size of the capital. Financing activities involve taking out loans, issuance of shares, paying dividends, etc. When a company extends credit to a customer, it is not a financial activity; it is an investing activity.

Cash flow related to repaying loans, borrowing, and issuing of shares is classified as cash flow from financing activities. Financing cash flow reveals the sale or purchase of stock in a company.

How to Calculate Cash Flow

In accounting, cash flow can be calculated by adjusting the net income. The operating cash flow is revealed in the statement of cash flow. The operating cash flow reflects the in-flow of cash during a particular period. There are two methods of calculating operating cash flow. These methods are direct and indirect.

The direct method derives information from the income statement by making use of cash disbursements and cash receipts. In the direct method, different kinds of payment received and made through cash are added. You can calculate these payments and receipts by making use of the balances of different business accounts.

In the indirect method, operating cash flow is calculated by deriving the net income from the income statement of an organization. Because the income statement of an organization is always made on an accrual basis, income is not recorded when it is received; it is recorded when it is earned. The indirect method is not a straightforward method of calculating operating cash flow.

The Importance of Cash Flow Statements

Investors are always concerned about the cash flow of an organization. Positive cash flow is a good sign for investors because this shows that the organization generates cash from its day-to-day operations. Operating cash flow can give a clear picture of an organization's profitability.

The purpose of preparing a statement of cash flow is to evaluate the sources of cash and how cash is utilized in a company over a particular period. The cash flow statement is one of the most important financial statements in accounting. Investors depend on this financial statement for making decisions because of its transparency.

The statement of cash flow helps to determine the solvency and liquidity of a business. It provides the necessary details for accessing a company's liabilities, assets, and equity. With the cash flow statement, businesses can determine the trends of their performance. This financial statement also predicts the timing and amount of cash flows in the future.

A business can only be successful if it has enough cash. Cash is needed to make business transactions like paying expenses, paying taxes, purchasing assets, and paying loans. With a cash flow statement, a business can determine the amount of cash available and how cash is generated and spent daily.

A business that lacks enough cash cannot make business transactions, and with time will go bankrupt. Without cash in a business, such businesses will need to borrow money to make some business transactions; this is not healthy for a business. The cash flow is useful in businesses and big organizations.

CHAPTER 10

THE INCOME STATEMENT ACCOUNT AND THE BALANCE SHEET

The income statement account and the balance sheets are one of the most important financial statements in accounting and bookkeeping. For all businesses, large or small, these financial statements are vital to evaluate and reflect your business's performance over a fiscal period. This chapter explains the uses of the income statement account and the balance sheet.

What is an Income Statement?

An income statement is a financial statement that reflects the profits, losses, income, and expenses of a business during a fiscal period. The income statement is also referred to as a profit and loss statement. The income statement is easy to understand since it states only the revenue and expenses accounts. This financial statement reflects the profitability of a business.

When revenues exceed expenses, the business is profitable. If expenses exceed revenue, the business is running at a loss.

The income statement is a crucial part of a business's financial statements. Used to list the income and expenses, it shows the net income and evaluates the business performance by analyzing non-operating and operating activities.

Investors use the income statement since it provides a clear picture of a business's profitability. This financial statement can influence investor's decisions. The income statements are required from large corporations because they provide users with the necessary details.

Why an Income Statement is Important

An income statement is important in businesses because of the following reasons:

Reflects the trends and patterns in business's finances. Since income statements are prepared monthly, quarterly, or yearly, companies can use them to compare past income statements with the present one. Comparison analysis can provide a great deal of information regarding the status of the company.

Provides a clear picture of a business's financial position: Income statements help businesses to determine their financial position. With this financial statement, you can easily know if your business is doing well or not.

Helps to make crucial decisions: The income statement is an important financial statement that helps business owners to make critical decisions. If your business is not doing well, you can plan strategies and make decisions that will improve your business's profitability.

Terms Used in Income Statements

Cost of Sales

The cost of sales states the cost of goods sold or services rendered by the business. Depreciation expenses are also included in the cost of sales. For businesses that produce goods, their cost of sales refers to the production of goods. It adds the expenses incurred from purchasing raw materials, labor, and manufacturing.

Retailers and wholesalers are also concerned about the cost of buying and reselling the products. Meanwhile, for businesses that render services, the cost of sales refers to the cost incurred from creating and rendering services to customers.

Net Sales

Net sales are the sales or income of a business. It reflects the sales of goods and services in a specified period. It reflects the profitability of a business.

Income Taxes

The income tax in the income statement is the estimation of income tax for the financial period.

Gross Income

It is also called gross margin or gross profit. The gross income is derived by calculating the difference between the cost of sales and net sales. Gross profit is the money available in a business that can be used to pay off expenses that might be incurred. The greater the gross profit, the more the net income.

Net Income

This is an important aspect of the income statement. The net income lists all operational and non-operational income and expenses and then calculates the difference. When income exceeds expenses, the business is running at a profit; if income is less than the expenses, the business is running at a loss.

Selling, General and Administrative Expenses

These expenses include the operational expenses incurred by the business. It reflects the business's efficiency. Business owners and investors are often more concerned about this aspect. If a business needs to cut its expenses, it considers the selling, general, and administrative expenses.

Operating Income

The operating income is derived by subtracting selling, general, and administrative expenses from the gross profit. Operating income is what the business can generate before deducting or adding any non-operating expenses.

Interest Expense

When a business borrows money, it will need to pay interest on the money borrowed. The interest expense refers to any interest payment made by the business.

Extraordinary Expenses

Sometime unexpected expenses arise in business. These occasional expenses need to be taken into account when planning a budget.

Understanding an Income Statement

There are certain things you need to know when analyzing and interpreting the income statement. The income statement will reveal everything about a business's profitability. As a business owner, accountant, and bookkeeper, you need to make sure the figures in this statement are accurate. Ensure your calculations are correct, because any mistake made will affect the evaluation of the business.

It is important to know the indicators that matter most and evaluate them carefully. One of the indicators that helps determine the profitability of a business is gross income. The operating income shows the efficiency of your business in terms of management. The net income is one of the major concerns for investors as it reveals the overall profitability of your business.

As a business owner or an investor, you might decide to compare the results of your income statement with another business that runs the same type of business. Comparing the income statements of business organizations can reveal how your business is performing in the industry.

Small businesses might find it difficult to have access to income statements of other similar businesses. Some businesses offer a financial statement that can give crucial information about the status of the company. The accounting methods adopted by businesses can influence the income statement. For instance, some businesses make use of the cash basis method, which records revenue when businesses receive cash.

There can be differences in the expenses section too. The way expenses are accounted for can influence the annual expenses of a business. When comparing and analyzing income statements, you must figure out where the different methods are utilized in order to have a better overview of the company.

The Balance Sheet

The balance sheet is one of the most essential financial statements in accounting. It is crucial to understanding the performance of a business. This financial statement reflects the net worth of a business. It is a financial statement that states the asset, liability, and equity of a business. The accounting equation: Assets = Liabilities + Equity is the basis of the balance sheet.

There are two main sides in the balance sheet: the right and the left side. The owner's equity, as well as the liabilities recording, are done on the right-hand side, while the left side takes an accounting of the company's assets. Assets are classified into fixed and current assets, while liabilities are current and long-term liabilities. This financial statement gives you a clear picture of your small business's financial position at a particular period.

The Structure of the Balance Sheet

The balance sheet follows a particular structure. There are several items included in the balance sheet. These items are explained below.

Current Assets

Cash and cash equivalents: In the balance sheet, assets are recorded on the left side. Cash, which is an example of current assets, is recorded first. Other assets recorded in this section include cash equivalents and other assets that are short term or assets that can be liquidated, like marketable securities.

Inventory: The inventory account involves the amounts for goods still in the production process, raw materials, and finished products. Inventories are goods manufactured or purchased by a company to be sold to customers. From the time of production to the time they are purchased by customers, it is known as inventory.

Accounts receivable: Accounts receivable refer to the amount debtors are yet to pay a business organization. It refers to the sales revenue that have not yet been received from customers or debtors.

Fixed Asset

Fixed assets are also known as non-current assets. They refer to the physical assets that a business owns. Fixed assets depreciate with time; therefore, when these assets are recorded, a depreciation amount is deducted from them.

Equipment, property, and plants: Property, equipment, and plants fall into this category. Examples include land, buildings, vehicles, and other types of equipment. Land is a good example of fixed assets that are owned for a longer period than other types of fixed assets. It is a type of fixed asset whose value does not depreciate but tends to appreciate over time.

Intangible Asset

Intangible asset refers to assets of a company that adds value to that company. Such assets are not easily valued. Examples include licenses, goodwill, patents, and secret formulas.

Current Liabilities

Current liabilities are also referred to as short term liabilities. These liabilities are obligations that have to be made within a short period of time.

Accounts payable: Accounts payable refer to the amount owed by a company. When a company buys stocks, items, or services on credit from another supplier, it is called account payable. This type of liability has to be paid back within a short term. When a business pays off its debt, the cash account decreases as well as the accounts payable.

Accrued expenses: These are listed as liabilities in the bookkeeping, but the due date has not come. Examples include wages, interest, etc.

Taxes payable: Many companies owe local, state and federal tax. When a business owes taxes that were meant to be paid to the government, it is called taxes payable. All taxes are classified as current liabilities since they are to be paid within a year.

Non-Current Liabilities

This is also called long term liabilities. This term refers to debts that will be due in more than a year. There are debts whose payments are extended over a long period. It refers to the amount of money a company owes a third party, and it becomes due to be paid for more than one year.

Bonds payable: Bonds payable refer to the number of bonds a company issues, and it is yet to be paid.

Long-term debt: This is also a good example of non-current liabilities. It is the total amount owed by a company, and it is not yet to be paid. This account is obtained from the debt schedule and reflects all the outstanding debt owed by a business.

Owner's Equity

This is also referred to as shareholder's equity. It is the amount of money that the business owner invests in the business. When a business starts, the owner will invest money for the smooth running of the business; such amount is called the owner's equity. It is derived by deducting total liabilities from total assets.

Retained earnings: This refers to the net income a business keeps. In every financial period, a business may decide to pay off dividends from the net income. The amount left is added to retained earnings. This also refers to the excess earnings kept back by the business.

How is the Balance Sheet Interpreted and Analyzed

The balance sheet is a financial statement used by business owners, investors, and financial analysts. A financial analyst can use this financial statement to derive financial ratios that will help to evaluate the financial performance of a business.

The changes in this financial statement can be used to derive cash flow in the statement of cash flow. For instance, a positive change in fixed assets like machinery, plant, and the property is equal to capital expenses less depreciation expense.

Importance of Balance Sheet

The balance sheet is a very vital financial statement in accounting. This section discusses the importance of the balance sheet in businesses.

It is an important document used by stakeholders, investors, and creditors to have an insight into the financial position of a business.

It can be used to make a comparison between organizations in the same sector; this will help to evaluate the growth of a business.

Since the balance sheet states the assets, liabilities, and equity of a business, it reveals the solvency and liquidity of a business.

By comparing the past and present balance sheet of an organization, it enables an organization to identify the pattern of growth. Identifying the pattern of growth helps the organization make decisions that will improve business activity.

It can be used to determine how a business generates returns. For instance, when the net income is divided into the owner's equity, it is Return on Equity (ROE).

When net income is divided into total assets, it generates Return on Assets (ROA).

- The analysis of the balance sheet can enable a business to undertake some projects and meet unplanned expenses.

- The balance sheet also helps to determine if a business is being funded with debt or profit. Hence, it reveals the profitability of a business.

The Difference Between the Income Statement and Balance Sheet

Although the income statement and the balance sheet are both financial statements, these two financial statements are different. The differences between these two statements are discussed below.

Items recorded: The income statement accounts for revenue and expenses that lead to calculating net gain or loss, while the balance sheet accounts for assets, liability, and shareholder's equity.

Uses: The income statement is used to evaluate the profitability of a business, i.e., if a business is running at a profit or loss. The balance sheet helps to evaluate the liquidity of a business.

Timing: the balance sheet reflects the financial position of a business at a particular period while the income statement reflects the results of a business for a longer period. For instance, financial statements for December will have a profit and loss statement for December and a balance sheet as of December 31.

Metrics: sales are compared with the subtotals in the profit and loss statement to generate the operating income percentage, gross profit percentage, and net income percentage. The different items recorded in the balance sheet are compared to determine a business's liquidity.

The balance sheet and the profit and loss statement are important to understanding how a business operates and determining the liquidity of a business. Small business owners can prepare the profit and loss statement as well as the balance sheet to check the growth of their businesses.

The structures of the balance sheet and the items reported in it have been explained in this chapter. The profit and loss statement are also easy to prepare. Regardless of the type or nature of your business, the income statement and the balance sheet are important.

CHAPTER 11

CASH FLOW MANAGEMENT IN SMALL BUSINESSES

Small businesses need to manage the flow of cash in their businesses, as this is a vital aspect of business management. This chapter discusses how cash, accounts payable and accounts receivable can be managed in small businesses.

What is Cash?

Cash is a very useful asset in a business, and it is the most liquid asset. It performs several functions in a business. No matter the type or nature of a business, cash is needed. Cash plays a significant role in running a business. Cash is used for the following purposes:

Transactions: Cash is used to make business transactions; without cash, no business transaction can be carried out. No matter the type of payments made, either by cash, checks, credit card, cash is always needed.

Security: Cash available in a business guarantees the security of the business. The amount of cash available in a business reflects its solvency.

Investment: No matter the type or nature of the investment, cash is needed for investments.

Cash is needed to meet the needs of a business. Most transactions carried out in businesses involve cash. Transactions that do not involve cash are non-financial. Business owners become more concerned when the cash available in the business is not enough to carry out business transactions. This is can be risky because most businesses that lack cash often end up taking out bank loans or borrowing from other businesses and going deeper into debt.

However, it is not only cash scarcity that occurs in businesses, but the surplus of cash is also a concern for businesses. Some businesses experience cash surplus, but they do not know what to do with the surplus.

It is financially unhealthy to leave cash surplus in accounts without investing it on something profitable for your business. Excess cash can generate income for your business if you use them wisely. Since cash is a liquid asset, it can be easily be converted and managed.

How to Use Excess Cash?

If you have excess cash in your business, it can be used for several things including:

Treasury Securities

The Treasury obligations of the United States is the biggest sector of the money market. Bonds are the primary securities issued here.

Commercial Paper

Commercial paper is a promissory note that has a fixed maturity. Financial organization and certain companies issue commercial paper. It can be bought through dealers or directly from the finance organizations. companies like CIT Financial Corporation sell commercial paper. Companies issue commercial paper at a discount.

Banker's Acceptances

These are drafts used in financing domestic and international trade. Banks accept these drafts, and their creditworthiness is determined by the acceptance of the draft by the bank. Banker's acceptances are traded in a market where few dealers dominate.

Agency Securities

The federal government has several agencies, and their duties are guaranteed by agency security. The Government National Mortgage Association (GNMA) and the Federal Housing Administration (FHA) are the primary agencies in charge of issuing securities. The securities issued are highly marketable.

Cash Inflow and Cash Outflow

What is Cash Inflow?

A business can generate cash through the sale of fixed assets, new debt, new investment, and operating income. The most reliable source of cash inflow is operating profits. The backbone of a business is the payment receipt from customers for rendering services or selling products. When customers make a payment for selling your products or services immediately, more cash will be generated in the business.

Cash can be managed efficiently when customers make a payment without delays. An example of this ideology is the fast-food industry. In the fast-food industry, payments are made by credit card or cash. Payments made by checks have to go through a process that can be time-consuming. It takes some time for banks to clear a check; therefore, payments made by check are not prompt payments.

The objective of cash management is to reduce the time it takes for funds to be transferred. Several techniques have been developed to speed up the check's clearance.

Lockboxes: A lockbox system can be used by businesses to collect payments. If you want to do this, you need to rent a post office box. Then you have to inform your bank to open the lockbox and credit your account directly.

Concentration banking: Large businesses can have wide market coverage. You can make use of banks at different locations to accelerate the process of clearing checks. This will help transfer funds faster.

The concentration of cash: When cash is concentrated in an account, it allows you to reduce cash reserves.

What is Cash Outflow?

Cash outflow refers to the amount of money disbursed by a business. It is the amount of money that leaves a business. It can be as a result of paying wages, paying dividends, and paying rent. When a business's cash outflow exceeds its inflow, this is financially unhealthy for such a business.

Cash outflows are a result of expenses incurred in the business. A business should ensure that it considers the type of demands it makes on its cash.

Cash Flow Budgets

You must prepare a cash flow analysis before you make a cash flow budget. A cash flow analysis helps you evaluate the inflow and outflow of cash in your business. A cash flow analysis gives you a clear picture of how your business operates. Small businesses need to understand how cash flows work. Small businesses are sometimes vulnerable to cash flow problems because they tend to perform business transactions with insufficient cash reserves or none.

Businesses must consider the time cash flows in and out. For instance, if a business spends cash in the first half of the year and generates cash in the second half of the year, it might fail before it is has a chance to receive cash inflows to operate well. Cash flow timing is very important in business.

Many small businesses fail to control the flow of cash. Preparing a cash flow budget is very important for businesses that want to control their cash flow. Businesses can get into trouble if they lack enough cash to pay their bills. Managing the flow of cash in your business is not a complex thing to do.

You only need some systematic approaches to control cash flow in your business. You need to do the following:

Determine the Sources of Cash In-Flows in Your Business

The sources of cash inflows include new debts and new investments. However, you cannot depend on these sources because they are not frequent. When you sell fixed assets, they are examples of new investments. Selling fixed assets are secondary to operating profits. For businesses, it is crucial to pay attention to operating profits.

Operating profits are not easy to track because they are ongoing. Therefore, businesses need to monitor their operating profits constantly. As your business grows, the need for cash will increase. For instance, when a business is experiencing fast growth, it will need to increase its inventory, cash transactions, and receivables. The process of increasing inventory will likely require large amounts of cash.

The period when businesses experience fast growth may be a challenging one. During these periods, receivables, inventories, etc. might consume all your gains. Some of these problems might result from extending payment terms to clients while you are being asked to pay suppliers within a short period.

Identify Cash Outflows

You can identify how cash is going out by checking the cash journal. It is important to identify where you are spending the cash. When disbursing cash in the business, it is important to ask questions like, "Is the expenditure necessary?" "Is the timing right?" "Can the expenditure be postponed?" If you cannot identify where you are spending cash, you need to consult an accountant. Small businesses can get enough details of cash disbursements from a checkbook.

Identify the Timing of Cashflow and Distribution

A calendar helps you to determine the timing of cash flow. Since most businesses prepare accounts yearly, you can examine your income and expenditures in a year. Before you do this, you need to make a list of cash outflow. List the items you have spent money on until you are certain that the list is complete. When you are done listing cash outflow, you can start listing cash inflow. This will give you a clear picture of cash flow timing.

Examine the Difference Between the Outflow of Cash and The In-Flow of Cash

When cash inflow exceed cash outflow, it is called a positive cash flow period. If a business experiences positive cash flow, such a business is successful. But this may not be the case at all times, as there are cases where cash outflow exceeds cash inflow. If a business experiences a negative cash flow period, it will need to source funds from other sources, such as a borrowing money from a bank.

Sometimes, negative cash flow occur in businesses, especially when growth spurts occur. Some businesses go through a period of sales rhythms. If this happens, observe the rhythm and the timing of cash inflow so that you can plan well for negative cash flow when it occurs.

Identify How the Present Cash Flow Affects the Business

One of the ways a business owner can regulate and improve cash flow is to reduce the outflow of cash while accelerating the inflow of cash. Before you do this, you need to evaluate the effects of slowing down payment to suppliers.

Identify the Sources of Outflow and Inflow Whose Timings Can be Altered

To prevent negative cash flow conditions, you can identify the cash outflow and cash inflow that can be altered. Sometimes, you need to discuss this with your creditors and decide on a payment schedule that is helpful to you. Some large companies and banks will agree on payment schedules as long as it benefits the parties involved.

If you inform your creditors that payment cannot be made at a particular period, they can reschedule their cash flow requirements.

Set Up a Strategy for Positive Cash Flow

A cash budget is a tool for planning positive cash flows. Cash budget refers to making plans for cash needs and cash receipts in the future. A cash budget reflects the amount and timing of cash that will be generated and disbursed over a specified period. For instance, most businesses prepare a budget for a year; you can prepare a two-year cash budget by making changes to the budget of the second year.

The cash budget should consider seasonal variations in cash flows. You need to know that the longer your cash flow budget is, your projections become more uncertain. The essence of a cash budget is to make plans for cash outflow and inflow that might occur in the future; the accuracy of your projection makes it useful.

How to Prepare Cash Budgets

To prepare cash budgets for a business, one needs to make sales projections. When generating a sales projection, you can ask the sales manager to forecast sales for the future. The sales manager observes the trends and patterns of sales in your business and then derives these estimates. This approach of making sales projections is the internal approach.

Since the internal approach may be too narrow, many businesses utilize the external approach of making sales projections. Some consulting organizations utilize an econometric modeling approach to estimate economic conditions. Another step you need to take when preparing a cash budget is to identify the cash receipts. The past trends of your credit and cash sales should be used to determine time delays.

CHAPTER 12

FINANCING YOUR SMALL BUSINESS

As a small business owner, you need to pay attention to your business financing. All businesses, whether large or small, needs finance; it is a vital aspect of a business. When talking about business financing, one needs to make a clear difference between new businesses and the ones that have existed for some time. This chapter talks about business financing and how small business owners can finance their businesses by going bankrupt.

What is Business Finance?

When we talk about business finance, we mean the money and credit channeled to a business for its smooth operations. It refers to acquitting and utilizing funds so that a business can perform day-to-day operations. Business finance involves all kinds of funds used for a business's operations. Regardless of the type, size, and nature of a business, finance is needed every time.

Finance is the lifeblood of a business; without it, no business can exist. The amount used for funding a business differs from one business organization to another based on the type, size, and nature of the business. Therefore, business finance has to do with the raising of funds, investment of funds, and estimation of funds.

One of the major problems small businesses face is the lack of funds. Some businesses have closed down because of a lack of funds. Running a business is not meant for people who are weak at heart, but for those who are willing to take a risk. Starting a business is a risk.

Small Business Financing

Most small businesses fund their business operations using traditional small business loans. These loans are useful when starting a business; it helps to build working capital and create cash flow. Small business financing may need to be funded by personal loans as well as small business loans. Small business owners need to be very careful when taking out a loan from entities because some may result in bad credit loans.

Large businesses have more access to financing than small businesses because large businesses tend to have more assets that are mostly used as collateral to secure loans. These assets can be sold off when the business cannot pay back any monies owed. Therefore, lenders always know that large businesses can look for ways to pay back the loan.

Larger businesses have more experience and longer operational history. Lenders always check the operating history of a business before considering granting it a loan. The operation history of businesses reveals a lot about the business because it reflects the profitability of the business and is the main reason lenders require for it before granting loans.

Although large businesses might have more opportunities to take out bank loans than small businesses do, there are several kinds of loans for small businesses too. Small business owners should not borrow large amounts of money to fund their businesses; this might be very risky, especially if it can't be paid back.

The Need to Finance a Business

For any organization, firm, or business to stand strong, it requires funding. Funds are required for the purchase of land, machinery, inventory, etc.

Money is also required for paying wages and salaries, utility bills, interest expenses, rents, telephone bills, etc.

BOOKKEEPING

In the business world, the process of production continues because goods or services will be demanded. Businesses will continue to incur expenses. Funds will help a business to achieve lots of things; for example, an organization might need to purchase computers to be installed in offices. In this case, funds are required.

Funds are needed to meet unforeseen expenses that might occur in businesses. Funds are also required to boost sales. A business organization might need to adopt strategies like home delivery service, advertising, personal selling, etc. to boost sales. Such a business needs money to accomplish these tasks.

Funds are also needed to make good use of business opportunities that may arise in businesses. Suppose there is a sales offer for a business, a supplier promises to give a 20% discount if it buys goods worth $150,000. This is considered a big opportunity for the business, but it will not be able to make good use of such an opportunity if it lacks funds.

Funds are needed to finance a business's inventory. Once a business organization is established, it needs money to manufacture its own goods or to purchase inventory. An organization invests a whole lot on purchasing or manufacturing inventory before it starts receiving payment for the inventory sold.

Types of Business Finance

One of the primary reasons businesses fail is lack of capital. It is not easy to run a business. In the financial year 2017/2018, more than 250,000 businesses failed. This can be a result of insufficient investment in operations. Therefore, you must choose the type of finance that is suitable for your business. This decision is critical to running a successful or a failed business.

A business can either be financed with debt or equity. Therefore, there are two primary types of business finance: equity finance and debt finance. A business is debt-financed when funds are borrowed from an external entity and paid back with interest, while a business financed with equity receives funds from the shareholder and use it to run a business.

What is Debt Financing?

In the financing world, a business is funded by debt when it borrows money from external parties with an agreement to pay back at a specified date. Small business loans, term loans, credit cards, and merchant cash advance are examples of debt financing. The loans granted to small businesses can be short term or long term.

The short-term loan spans 30 days to 12 months, while long term loans span one year to five years. If your business is financed by debt, your business is still owned by you, unlike equity financing that affects the ownership of your business.

Before an institution or entity can grant you a loan, the creditworthiness of your business will be evaluated by lenders. They will consider the financial records of your business, your operation history, credit rating, ability to pay back the loan, and if you have invested in the business. Debt financing has its advantages and disadvantages.

Pros:

- You have absolute control over your business.

- You have the capital to start your business with an agreement to pay back at a specified date.

- The loan can either be a short term or long-term loan.

- It is suitable for business owners as there are many sources of debt financing.

- The loans' interest is tax-deductible.

Cons:

- You have to pay back the loan at a specified time.

- The repayments of the loan start immediately after the loan approval.

- Cash inflow needs to be sufficient and steady to pay back at the agreed time.

- There is a probability that the business might not be able to pay back due to some unexpected happenings.

- The loan is always granted and secured against collateral.

- The business might not be able to grow again because the loan repayment drained some cash.

Sources of Debt Finance

There are various sources of debt finance; the primary sources are explained below.

Retailers: You can finance your business by buying goods on credit for your business. Several small businesses do that. Some retailers are ready to offer you goods with no interest.

Relatives or friends: Your family member(s) or friends can offer you a loan with an agreement that you will repay it at a particular date.

Financial institutions: These include credit unions and banks. They can provide you with lines of credit, bank overdrafts, and loans. Banks offer to provide funds for your business by granting loans to you. The bank offers you a particular amount of money with an agreement to repay the loan over a specified period.

A line of credit is like a credit card that provides a facility that you can use when you need it and pay it back on an agreed term. Business owners can have issues in getting a line of credit or a bank loan. The bank is only interested in being repaid with interest. Banks grant loans and expect borrowers to pay interest on the loan.

Finance companies: Finance companies provide loans to businesses.

Peer-to-peer lenders: This kind of entity matches people who need loans with people who have funds to invest. Loans granted have to be paid back within a specific period, and the rates of interest differ based on the level of risk involved.

Factor companies: Factoring is a process in which a business organization sells its accounts receivable to a third entity, which is referred to as a factor to receive funds without having to wait for customer payment. Invoices are paid by customers to the factoring company directly.

Invoice financing: This happens when your invoices are exchanged for upfront cash that is equal to a percentage of the value of your invoice. This is ideal for your business if it struggles with the differences between payment and invoices.

Trade finance: This is a type of finance that is utilized for the facilitation of exports and imports.

What is Equity Financing?

Equity financing is when a third-party investor is funding a business, and a percentage of that business is bought or owned by the investor. The investor offers you the capital needed, and he has a share in the profit earned in the business. The investor can also take part in the decision-making process.

For the investor, equity financing comes with a high level of risk. If the business fails, the investor will be paid back. There are several factors to consider in equity financing, and this includes voting rights, decision making, dilution, and the valuation and exit methods. Equity financing comes with some benefits and disadvantages:

Pros:

- It involves less risk since the amount invested need not be repaid immediately.

- There will be more cash available in the business since you don't need to pay back a loan.

- The skills and credibility of investors can be favorable to your operation.

- Funds can be raised at an early stage without having an operating history, unlike loans that require the profitability of a business or its operating history.

Cons:

- The ownership of your business is affected as investors take a share of your business's ownership.

- Investors take part in the decision-making process.

- The process of getting investors who will be interested in your business is time-consuming and challenging. It requires legal considerations and intricate contracts.

Sources of Equity Finance

The primary sources of equity finance include the following:

Venture capital: This is a type of business that deals with investing in businesses in whom they see profits and potentials.

Government: Sometimes, the government encourages small business owners by granting them funds to start their businesses. This can come in the form of information and guidance and low cost or free advisory services.

Private investors: Private investors are called 'business angels.' These "angels" are wealthy and invest a large amount of money in businesses to have a share of the profits as well a share of the ownership.

Family or friends: Your family member(s) or friends can fund your business in exchange for taking a share of your business profits and ownership. You need to be careful in accepting this offer as it may result in creating an unhealthy relationship with your friends or family.

Crowdfunding: This refers to raising funds via the collective endeavors of a group of people. Examples include crowdfunding platforms or social media. It allows investors to offer a large amount of money in return for profit or ownership.

Personal finances: This is very common in small businesses. When the business owner decides to fund the business from her personal assets or personal savings, it is personal finance. Business owners are advised against using home loans, retirement savings, and insurance loans to fund risky businesses.

Angel investors: These set of people are interested in investing in a profitable business by purchasing equity. They can provide funds, advice, and expertise to help you start a business and make it grow. Angel investors are very hard to come by because they always require evaluating the profitability and viability of a business plan.

They always have an exit plan. An exit plan is a strategy that allows investors to get their money back and take their profits. Often, these investors operate on a limited time frame, which can be within three to five years.

Types of Finance

The types of finance in this section are defined based on the duration period of its operating cycle, and its purpose. There are three types of finance - short-term, medium-term, and long-term.

Short-Term Finance

Short-term finance is for use within a year. This type of finance is needed for financing the daily operations of a business.

Medium-Term Finance

Businesses use this finance for more than a year, but not more than five years. The medium-term finance is needed for renovation, repair, and modernization of machinery.

Long-Term Finance

Long-term finance has a duration of about five years or more before being repaid. This type of finance is needed for financing and the purchase of non-current or fixed assets such as machinery, land, vehicles, etc.

CHAPTER 13

CLOSING THE BOOKS FOR YEAR-END

In bookkeeping and accounting, a business has to close its books for the year-end. At the beginning of the year, different financial statements are prepared, and at the end of the year, these accounts and statements need to be closed. This chapter discusses how books are closed for the year-end.

What Does a Closing Process Mean?

A closing process in accounting refers to the steps an accountant must take to review and zero out some accounts, like the income and expenses accounts, and then record the net profit or loss in the balance sheet. If you use accounting software to prepare your books, it will close your revenue and expense accounts automatically.

Most times, the closing process is always carried out by an accountant. However, a small business owner can use accounting software to accomplish this task. Your books need to be closed annually since you need to file income tax returns every year. It is a common practice among businesses to close their books monthly.

If you perform many transactions and your business is large, you might need to leave the closing process to your accountant. As a business owner, you should understand the process of closing the books, even if you are not doing it yourself. This will help you to know if your job was well done.

Closing your books for the year-end means that all your reports have been finalized. These reports reveal the financial performance of a business during an accounting period. Business owners are entitled to know the ups and downs of their business.

Closing entries are aspects of the accounting process that occur at the end of an accounting period. During the closing process, balances in temporary accounts are posted to permanent ones. These temporary accounts include dividends, income, and expense accounts.

Why You Need to Close Your Books

There are different reasons you need to close your books. The main purpose of closing the books is to ensure that revenue generated and expenses incurred from a previous accounting year are not carried over to the current account year. The closing process also helps business owners have insight into the financial position of their business.

Small business owners should ensure that their books are closed at the end of the year to file income tax returns annually. When you close your books, you can easily detect any error in your bookkeeping and accounting system. Closing the books also help businesses prepare for the next accounting period.

When you close your books monthly, it makes it easier to carry out monthly tasks such as paying your suppliers, sending invoices to customers, reconciling bank statements, preparing the journal, and sending reports on sales tax to the state. The closing process also helps you create an outline and strategies for the next accounting period.

Steps You Need to Take When Closing the Books

Transfer Entries in the Journal to the General Ledger

The journal is the first book where transactions are recorded. Entries in the journal need to be posted to the general ledger. The closing process requires you to record the account totals from your cash receipts and payments in the general ledger. Cash payments involve all transactions paid with cash or checks.

Add Up All Accounts in the General Ledger

This is the second step you need to take when you are closing the books. Sum up all the transactions in every general ledger account. For instance, you can sum up all entries in the expense account.

Prepare a Preliminary Trial Balance

A trial balance is a financial report that calculates all debits and credits of your accounts. Ensure the debits and credits are balanced and if it is not the case, recheck your work to correct the errors.

Adjusting Entries

Adjusting entries keep track of items that are not recorded as daily transactions. These items are accrual of depreciation, accumulation of taxes.

Adjust the Trial Balance Again

Add up all accounts in your general ledger again to check the adjusting entries and total them to prepare a new trial balance.

Make Financial Reports

If you discover out that the total credits and debits are the same in your trial balance, then you can prepare your profit and loss statement and balance sheet. You can prepare these financial reports with your accounting software. Accounting software makes the preparation of financial statements easier and faster.

Make Closing Entries

This step requires you to zero your income and expense accounts and then enter the net loss of income to the owner's equity. Closing entries record the balances of these accounts to permanent accounts. For instance, the income account is cleared out and transferred into the retained earnings account.

Create a Post-Closing Trial Balance

Creating a post-closing trial balance is the last procedure in closing the books for the year-end. The difference between post-closing trial balance and other trial balances is that the balance in the expense and income accounts must be zero. To decide the amount of income and expenses for a particular period, one needs to begin with a zero balance in the expense and income accounts.

The trial balance will only include the balance sheet since all expenses and income accounts have been cleared out. Ensure that the credit and debit balances are the same in your prepared trial balance.

What You Need to Consider When Closing Your Books

There are several things you need to take into account when closing your books. The steps on how to close your books has been discussed above, but you need to know some things about closing your books.

Reconciliation of your bank account: Ensure that the balance on your books is the same with your final financial reports, especially if you have been recording transactions by hand. Remember, humans make mistakes. Be certain that all credit cards, money accounts, and bank statements are reconciled properly.

If you utilize accounting software make sure you crosscheck all the figures. If you want to be sure that your bank accounts are reconciled, you can employ a team of experts to make the work less stressful for you.

Evaluate Invoices and Accounts Receivable

Be certain that your invoices at the end of the year are cleared, and all invoices sent out are remunerated. Sent invoices can go unnoticed due to several tasks been performed at the year-end. This can lead to errors in your books. Therefore, you need to pay attention to all the details and make sure all transactions are well recorded.

Check Income Statements and Payroll Expenses

During the closing process, ensure that your annual and monthly payroll expenses are balanced. You need to check income statements and payroll expenses before filing your yearly taxes.

If you fail to deal with payroll expenses properly, you can be penalized by the IRS. Also, you need to have a careful study of your income statements to ensure that it is well arranged. You can seek help from a professional if you are not certain about your payroll taxes.

Fixed Assets and Depreciation Expenses

Things you need to take into account are your depreciation expenses and fixed assets when closing your book for the year-end. If you purchased any fixed assets, make sure you keep good track of them in your balance sheets. Deal with problems associated with depreciation during the closing process. This can be a little bit tricky and might need the skill of a professional.

The Accounts Affected by Closing Entries

Closing entries affect some accounts like revenue accounts, dividend accounts, and expense accounts. These accounts are cleared out when closing entries. Closing entries alter these accounts so that they don't change the next accounting period.

The balances of these accounts are recorded in retained earnings, which is not a temporary account. Sometimes, income and expenses are posted to an income summary, while dividends are posted to retained earnings.

CONCLUSION

You can only evaluate the performance of your businesses if you practice the art of bookkeeping and accounting. Bookkeeping and accounting help to organize your finances and evaluate your business's performance. As a business owner, you must have a financial understanding of how your business operates. A good bookkeeping and accounting system helps you to plan for the future.

Accounting and bookkeeping are very vital for operating a business. They are used in many organizations, and their principles apply to daily business operations. Every business spends money and makes sales, and with accounting and bookkeeping, it is easy to track these transactions. Regardless of the type or size of your business, accounting and bookkeeping play a significant role.

QUICKBOOKS

A Beginner's Guide to Bookkeeping and
Accounting for Small Businesses

By Michael Kane

INTRODUCTION

Owning a business requires certain financial obligations. Your main goal is to make money to keep the business running, pay for goods, expenses, employees and yourself. You have state and federal responsibilities too, such as federal and state taxes, employment taxes, sale taxes and incorporation fees (depending on the size and type of business).

Your obligations tell you to keep as much money in the business as possible, while meeting your financial responsibilities. Spending too much on expenses, such as occasional business needs, can decrease the amount of money you have for the more important expenses and bills.

Hiring an accountant who is a bookkeeper and accountant is one choice. The person fulfills the main functions for the financial responsibilities your company has. You can decide to have a bookkeeper that comes in once a week to take care of the daily, weekly, and monthly tasks, and have an accountant for the tax liabilities. For example, the accountant would file the yearly tax data and create the W-2 forms for employee tax information.

A third choice is for you to be the bookkeeper or have a staff member do part-time bookkeeping responsibilities and have an accountant to call for the important business financial questions and obligations.

If you plan on doing most of the bookkeeping in-house, whether someone comes in once a week or a staff member you already have takes care of the little things, then using accounting software, with bookkeeping capabilities is the perfect solution.

Prior to the 1980s, most bookkeeping was done by hand, using ledgers, notebooks and other manual concepts. With the invention of a more affordable computer, word processor concepts where you could create spreadsheets became the norm. One company decided to go further and create a program that would handle bookkeeping tasks and be useful for accountants. The company, Intuit, is behind QuickBooks and is the topic of discussion.

QuickBooks can be added when you start a business, to an existing business, or when you decide to switch from a different accounting and bookkeeping software. You might have used Quicken, Money, or something else that exists, so learning how to use QuickBooks and who it is meant for is going to help you decide if you want to use the program.

You are going to learn:

1. What QuickBooks is.
2. How it works.
3. Why you want to use it.

4. Its affordability.
5. The various tasks it helps with.

As you continue through the guide, you will gain:

- Step by step instructions.
- Knowledge for how to perform an every day task up to occasional duties.
- Tips for quick usability.

By the end, you will understand whether you want to buy or download the program, use it online, and how much time and money it is going to save you. You are also going to know if switching to QuickBooks or adding it new is the right method for your company. You have a lot of decisions to make, including how you want to learn to use the program. Thank you for choosing this comprehensive guide to business and the implementation of QuickBooks.

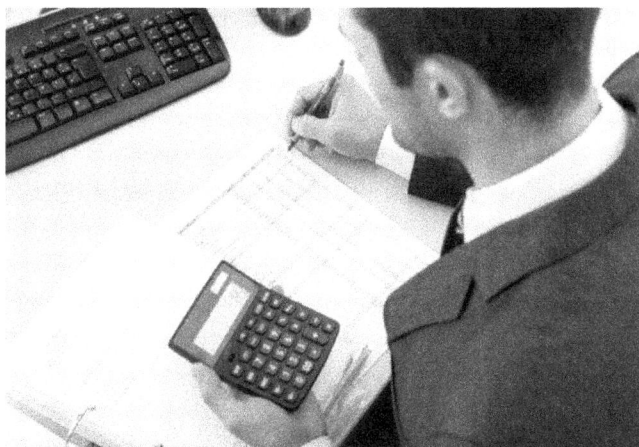

CHAPTER 1

QUICKBOOKS, ACCOUNTING AND BOOKKEEPING

Starting a business or taking over an older business that may not be up on its technology will require you to understand the various tools you can use to help you successfully run your company. QuickBooks is one way you can perform bookkeeping and accounting duties when running a business.

What is QuickBooks?

QuickBooks is a business software for the financial responsibilities your company has. You can do bookkeeping and accounting with QuickBooks software. Some businesses use the software only for paying their employees, while others use the full repertoire available.

QuickBooks is designed mostly for the small business retailer, contractor, manufacturer or distributor. It is also helpful for attorneys, non-profits and CPAs. The businesses that get the most use out of QuickBooks have under 50 employees, with less than $20 million in revenue.

History of QuickBooks

In 1494, Luca Pacioli invented a double-entry bookkeeping concept, which became known throughout the world. Pacioli was not the first to have bookkeeping and accounting practices. However, he was the first to describe the debits and credits concept. Pacioli used debits and credits in journals and ledgers, which we still have today. By 1887, accounting became a profession with the first CPAs licensed in 1896. Large firms started adding accountants on retainer, having accountants audit the books for performance and other reasons. Eventually, we hit a point where technology became useful beyond what Pacioli and early accountants could have imagined.

QuickBooks is part of Intuit's software line, founded in 1983 by Scott Cook and Tom Proulx. The first program they created was called Quicken. Quicken is still around today. While some functions are similar to QuickBooks, it is also meant for larger businesses. In 1992, they launched QuickBooks, which has become the most popular accounting software a small company can have. At the outset, QuickBooks had some limiting factors in what it could do and was unable to work with complex businesses. Many small businesses found tracking vendors, writing checks, paying employees and keeping up with accounts payable and receivable was doable with the software package. In 2001, QuickBooks gained new updates that made it worthwhile and, in 2015, it became the most used accounting software for small businesses.

QuickBooks has evolved from the 1992 version. At first, you had to buy the program and install it on your computer. It came in a box, with a manual and a disc. It is available in this way today, although the manual is now online. In the new millennium, QuickBooks, like many software companies, started offering the program via download from their website. It has evolved even further to be a program you access without downloading to your computer. The plans and pricings discussed later explain the CD-ROM option, download from the net, and online usage.

Intuit never stops trying to improve their accounting software. They offer continual updates and add new features that their clients will find useful.

Difference between Bookkeeping and Accounting

Bookkeeping is the recording of financial transactions. A bookkeeper is a person who enters in the data, maintains the current information, creates reports if necessary, but overall makes sure everything is recorded. Accounting is where the interpretation, classification, analysis, reporting and summation of financial data occurs. Accountants take the records created by the bookkeeper to create cash flow, taxes, employee paychecks and help show the financial health of the company through the analysis of the reports.

For a business to succeed bookkeeping and accounting must be done. How you set this up will determine the amount paid out for services, versus what you keep in-house. The size of your company also weighs in on the choice you make to have an accountant prepare documents or whether you prepare everything yourself. You are never going to be an accountant doing your taxes as a business, even if you have QuickBooks, but you can create as much data and reports as possible and handle small accounting concepts, without paying a large sum to an accountant.

Many small businesses have an accountant to do the taxes and create the W-2 forms for employee tax season. Otherwise, the owners take care of making payments, creating reports, interpreting the data for the next year projections, and other financial requirements.

Accountants work on an hourly basis, many charging over $100 per hour for their services. Imagine if you have an accountant who creates the paychecks on a bi-monthly timeframe, pays the sales tax, and employee taxes. Let's say it takes an hour for each task, so you pay out $400 per month. What if you could save that money, and only pay out $100 each month?

Why is Accounting Software Essential?

Accounting software is essential for a multitude of reasons the least of which is ensuring your company has proper accounting records for tax season. Accounting software can streamline your financial process to ensure you are tracking the success of your business, paying companies and employees on time, and providing a clear picture of your business' financial health. It is possible to not have an accounting software in-house, if you have hired an accountant. However, you can save yourself a lot of time and expense by having accounting software at the company to record everything.

The benefits of accounting software include:

- Accuracy – you can reduce human error in calculations.
- Speed – using software helps you become faster at the financial data you require.

- Cost – the software is often less expensive than hiring an accountant to do much of your financial work. Remember the example of $100 versus $400 per month?

- Reports – nearly all cash flow reports you might need, including what vendors have not been paid or accounts have not paid, can be tracked.

- Tax – taxes not only for employees, but also for your business can be calculated using the software. You can use the software to complete your income taxes with less spent on an accountant.

Excel Spreadsheet vs. Accounting Software

Old-school methods from when computers were just starting to be used, include using an excel spreadsheet to generate reports, keep track of employee payments, and more. While it might work when you have a couple of employees, a few vendors, or just sell services, it is much easier to use accounting software. Excel spreadsheets require you to lock certain columns, understand how Excel works, and create your own formulas.

For example, you would need to keep a ledger of incoming and outgoing funds. You would also need:

- A template for employee hours, taxes, net, and gross earnings to calculate your tax liability and create paychecks.
- A template for vendors.
- A vendor file with address, returns information, and contact information.

The list can go on. You would need to manually create all these things, save them in proper folders, and find them again when you need to work with the Excel sheets you create. It takes time. It takes effort. It is more work than using accounting software that keeps everything tidy.

Accounting software, like QuickBooks, does everything for you without the time and thought process spent on creating what you need.

As you buy a business or start a company, you need to ask yourself if you want to work smarter or harder. Tools that take less time to perform necessary actions ensure you are working smarter. With QuickBooks you have more time to work on bringing money in than bookkeeping and accounting concepts.

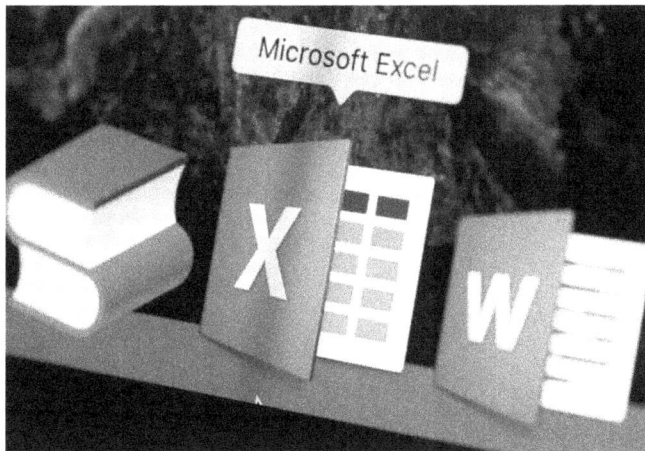

CHAPTER 2

WHY DO BUSINESSES USE QUICKBOOKS?

QuickBooks is not the only accounting and bookkeeping software on the market. However, small businesses have discovered it has numerous benefits beyond other software options. It is designed for small companies who often do not have the funds to hire a bookkeeper and accountant. QuickBooks is also easier to learn and integrate into a business than other software programs out there. While this last fact is an opinion, having used Quicken and QuickBooks, there are simple features in QuickBooks that are more complicated in Quicken. How the program works, how easy it monitors cash flow, customer support from QuickBooks, and the training provided by the company all make QuickBooks worth using.

QUICKBOOKS

How It Works

QuickBooks allows you to perform business tasks relating to bookkeeping and accounting. Some of the tasks you need to do occur daily, while others are less frequent. The program takes the information you provide regarding revenue and expenses, allocates information to certain customers and vendors, while keeping track of the bills that are outgoing and incoming. From the information supplied, QuickBooks maintains your bank account balances to show you how much money you have in the bank, and what needs to be spent. You can also draft reports to overview the financial health of your company. The following information breaks down the three parts to help your understanding of how QuickBooks works for businesses.

You can break QuickBooks into three parts:

- Daily Tasks
- Occasional Tasks
- Housekeeping Procedures

Daily Tasks

Daily tasks are the everyday items you take care of for bookkeeping.

- Creating Invoices
- Creating Credit Memos
- Payments
- Paying Bills
- Inventory
- Checkbook Details
- Paying Electronically

Each business has a need to create invoices. Invoices are sent out to those with accounts, such as a library picking up books on account, at a bookstore, and then paying their bill.

Businesses also send out credit memos when an overpayment or issue has occurred.

For payments, you typically send out invoices, but sometimes you need to keep on top of the company to ensure you get paid. You can also use QuickBooks as a Point of Sale system depending on your company's goods and services. You can use it to take payments for services or goods.

QuickBooks keeps track of the bills you pay and the bills that are becoming due. When you get an invoice or packing slip from a company for goods you bring in, QuickBooks can keep track of the payment terms and alert you to a payment needing to be made, as well as keep track in your check register of the payments you have made.

Furthermore, if you have a company where you make payments online for goods or services, you can use QuickBooks to send payments or even to take payments using electronic means or credit cards.

Occasional Tasks

On occasion, your business will have things that need to be done like printing checks. You probably don't send out payments each day, so these tasks are more about the weekly or monthly options.

- Printing Checks
- Payroll
- Creating the Budget

Printing checks is often a thing you will do once a week, and then twice monthly for payroll. Creating a budget is also something you do once a quarter and a yearly basis, which means you need to know that you can use QuickBooks for these tasks and how it works.

Housekeeping

These are chores you do occasionally, most often for accounting needs and business health.

- Balancing the check register
- Reporting, such as sales tax and other taxes
- Job Estimating, Billing, and Tracking
- File Management
- Fixed Assets and Vehicle Lists

When you get your bank statement, you reconcile your check register with the information on the bank statement. You also have sales tax and other taxes to pay or report about monthly.

QuickBooks is available to help you estimate job expenses, employment needs, billing and tracking of those jobs.

As with any business, you need hard copies of the files and a way to manage the different vendors, suppliers, customers and sales. These are housekeeping concepts when it comes to making sure your files are up-to-date.

Fixed asset and vehicle list maintenance is something you do when a new asset is purchased, an old one is sold or disposed of, and when you add new vehicles or trade out old ones. Your company needs a list of the assets; particularly, for the valuation and depreciation of them.

These are just a few of the topics that help you understand how QuickBooks works to provide you the information you need to perform daily, monthly, and housekeeping business tasks.

Cash Flow Monitoring

QuickBooks is also designed to help you track the cash flow you have. In several ways, you can print reports to show how much money is coming in and how much is going out. You can create reports that show where the money is going. From the cash flow monitoring reports, you also get suggestions from online support or through your accountant. These suggestions help you improve or streamline your company, so you are handling the cash flow better.

Customer Support

QuickBooks is something you can learn on your own. You are reading a guide to help you with the basic information, such as how to set up payroll, but you also have Intuit support through phone and chat that helps train you for the various tasks you want to perform. Customer support is based on the level of QuickBooks plan you buy. Simple questions can be answered without a support plan. For those who want more, such as training classes, and hands-on computer help you may want to pick a QuickBooks plan that includes more hands-on customer support.

Training Classes

Not everyone can read a book and learn everything they need to know. Sometimes it also helps to have personal training to streamline the process and cut out the details you don't need to know when it comes to QuickBooks. The training classes provided can be live, self-paced, or through personal support chats.

For customer support concepts, more details are coming with regard to the level of support based on the fee you pay for the QuickBooks program. You also have different options when it comes to training employees who may use the software to help you in the office. As more topics surface, the information will be discussed. The idea is whether you are the owner of the company or the one doing bookkeeping/accounting tasks with QuickBooks, you can use the information here to help you.

CHAPTER 3

PICKING THE RIGHT QUICKBOOKS PLAN

There are two main ways you can add QuickBooks to your store:

1. Online
2. CD-ROM

It is important to choose the right choice for you with regard to your accounting needs. Some businesses want the CD versus an online version. The benefits they require are minor compared to the options with online plans and pricing.

CD-ROM Choices

For a one-time payment, you can purchase QuickBooks, either in CD-ROM form or downloaded from the online website. It installs on your desktop and is accessed without the need of an Internet connection. The cheapest version is QuickBooks Pro. It is designed to help you maximize tax deductions, organize expenses, track business performance, gain financial, sales and tax reports, and you do not need accounting knowledge to use it. It will not come with unlimited customer support. You can ask a few questions when you set it up, but mostly you will need to refer to books like this to help you get through the daily, occasional and housekeeping tasks.

The Pro Plus option provides everything the Pro version has and adds unlimited customer support, automated data back-up with recovery options and software upgrades. When a new company begins or is transitioning into the online world, you can also add on hosting services, which help you update your online information, keep in touch with your account, and you don't need to pay for servers or IT maintenance with the hosting add-on. The Pro Plus is an annual subscription.

Now, you can gain even more if you are willing to pay a high price. An annual subscription to Enterprise 19.0 offers software that one to thirty people can use, with six times the capacity of the other programs, increased tools for reporting, inventory, and pricing, plus access to the QuickBooks Priority Circle Program. The Enterprise version is a point of sale concept, which is why it has an annual subscription, even though you can buy it as a CD-ROM version.

Most software programs, even Microsoft Word are digital, where you download the file directly from Microsoft's website. The need for CD-ROMs is ending, but that is not going to change the fact that for the Pro version you can pay once and use the software for years.

The pricing can change. In fact, as the details were being researched on Intuit, the pricing showed a discount for the payment options. If you walk into an office store to buy software or go online, you will see similar pricing.

- Pro - $299.95 once
- Pro Plus - $299.95 annually
- Enterprise 19.0 - $1155 annually

Plans and Pricing

If you decide to go with an online plan, you will pay a monthly fee. The plans are as follows.

1. Freelancer: a plan for the self-employed, which is normally $10 per month. It allows you to track income and expenses, capture and organize receipts, estimate quarterly taxes, invoices and accept payments, run basic reports and track your vehicle miles.

2. Advanced: a plan for $150 per month. It does everything the freelancer plan will do, but adds maximizing your tax deductions, running advanced reports, sending estimates, tracking sales and sales tax, managing bills, and it can support up to 25 individual users. You also get to track time, project profitability, inventory, and manager freelancers. It has smart reporting, quick invoicing, custom permissions, and Premium Care with Priority Circle.

3. Plus: for $60 per month, you can do everything the self-employed option gives you, along with maximizing tax deductions, running advanced reports, sending estimates, managing bills, tracking sales tax and sales, time, project profitability, and inventory. You can also manage freelancers and have up to 5 users.

4. Essentials: you do not have added customer support with essentials, but it can do everything the Plus does, except only up to three users can use the program. It is $35 per month.

5. Simple Start: it is like the freelancer except it helps with tax deductions, sales, sales tax, and sending estimates all for $20 a month.

All the plans have customer support, receipt capture, and app integration. You can also add other services such as self-service payroll, full-service payroll, on the plus, essentials and simple start programs. The advanced program has payroll options within the product for sale.

The freelancer choice does not have payroll and cannot be upgraded.

Pricing can change. Discounts may be available.

With the above plans and pricing, you can login to QuickBooks online or download it to the desktop. You can always upgrade your plan by paying the upgraded monthly fee. You are not under any contract. While miles are tracked with the Freelancer option, it is not fully integrated as a mileage tracking option. QuickBooks is hoping to add mileage tracking to their plans, with more features. If you use the mobile apps, you do not pay extra.

When you visit Intuit to add QuickBooks to your business, you can search by:

- QuickBooks Online – these are the above plans discussed.
- QuickBooks Self Employed – an added feature to the self-employed option is adding TurboTax to the bundle, where you gain options to pay your estimated taxes directly from QuickBooks, transfers to TurboTax, and federal/state returns each year. A secondary option with TurboTax bundle is to pay a little more and get help from a CPA.
- Online Advanced – the plus and advanced packages from above.

- Desktop for Mac – the download, using a one-time payment. It is not a plan, but the software.

- Desktop Pro – the software download discussed as CD-ROM options.

- Desktop Premier – software downloads with one time or annual subscriptions depending on the features you wish to have. It is more advanced in business features, including more for industry specific companies, creating sales orders, and setting product and service prices. You can buy the Premier, Premier Plus, or Enterprise versions.

- QuickBooks Point of Sale – designed as more than a bookkeeping and accounting system, the POS allows you to accept credit card payments, ring sales, track inventory, set up customer programs, sync with the accounting software from QuickBooks, and work with Microsoft Surface Pro systems.

Size and Type of Business

The size and type of business you are running will determine which QuickBooks program will work best for you. QuickBooks is designed for many types of businesses, but it tends to work with certain industries better such as contractors, attorneys, and manufacturers.

For a point of sale system, it is very broad and not set up for some of the industry specific choices like selling books in a bookstore. It is more for retail such as clothing.

The size of your business matters because these programs are set up for under 50 users. Typically, a small business needs the program on their main computer for bookkeeping and accounting. However, if you have sales representatives selling your products, you may need to have access for all employees so they can look at the inventory and proceed with an order. You want to make sure that your QuickBooks plan supports the number of users you have or will potentially have soon.

For businesses, with a bookkeeper who comes in twice a week to manage payments, payroll, and other daily activities, buying the CD-ROM or downloading it for a one-time payment can be enough. It also gives you everything your accountant will require. When you need more support and features, it can be time to turn to the plans and pricings discussed where you pay a monthly fee. There is one reason to pay for the downloaded version and save it to your hard drive, versus logging in each month to an online program. If your Internet is interrupted, you can still work with QuickBooks, where you cannot if you only have online access.

Now you have an understanding that the plans, pricing, and options for adding QuickBooks to your company are diverse. It is up to you to research further details based on your company needs, speak with customer service about the product that is right for you, and get started.

CHAPTER 4

TRAINING AND CUSTOMER SUPPORT

Intuit provides an "Intuit QuickBooks Community" and blog section for general customer support. It is available online. You also have "help" offline in the CD-ROM or download versions. Beyond Intuit, there are training courses provided by companies who partner with Intuit. These companies offer classes with certification. There are live training classes where you can go to a two-day seminar to learn how to use QuickBooks. You also have the webinar study for self-paced learning. We will examine the different options to help you decide the level of customer support you want from Intuit and whether you wish to also include training classes.

In-House Customer Support

If you find you are not getting answers from the "help" section in the downloaded version or you have the online version, you can go to the QuickBooks Community, and launch the support articles. The topics include:

- Getting Started
- Banking and Bank Feeds
- Account Management
- Reports and Accounting
- Income and Expenses
- Payments
- Employees and Payroll Taxes
- Inventory and Projects
- Apps
- Help Articles

You also have access to the blog. The blog offers timely articles that may not fit your needs. For example, one topic was about foreign currency transfers, and another was 8 free tax resources for small businesses. If you don't accept foreign currency, then it may not be of use to you. However, most companies want to save on tax resources, so there is something useful.

Online at QuickBooks, you can also launch the QuickBooks Tutorials section. It is broken into two departments, Small Business and Accountants. For the business user, the following are videos you can watch:

- What are QuickBooks Apps?

- Reconcile Your Accounts
- Add a User
- Export Company File to QuickBooks
- Online Banking Overview

Please note, there are dozens of videos. They are broken into topics from general accounting to invoicing, sales, taxes, and more.

Additional resources include Webinars, Resource Center and Support. The resource center offers guides, tools, and articles on starting and running a successful business. QuickBooks support provides help with any topic and any QuickBooks product.

The accounting tab also provides several videos and tutorials you may find useful, even if you are not an accountant. Such topics include introduction to QuickBooks online Self-Employed, using the accounting toolbox, using trial balance and more.

If you pay for it, you can call QuickBooks or start a live chat with a professional. You would click the live chat option while logged in to your QuickBooks program. If you are trying to order products or set up two or more bank accounts with QuickBooks, you can ask live chat questions and get it set up, without paying extra. It is after the setup and more in-depth questions you may have that require paying for the customer support services. But, remember you have books and online video guides to walk you through almost anything you might need to know.

Live Classes and Self-Paced Training

Intuit partners with at least one company. They endorse the training provided in a two-day live class in most large cities. The training is comprehensive. You are in a classroom setting, you get your questions answered, and you gain tips and tricks to help you work with the program. The training is set up as desktop or online training, where you go to a classroom with your computer.

You can also sign in via webinar, if there is not a class in your local area. If you want to take the training to the next level, you can go to the class, prepare for an exam, and then take an exam at a land-based location. The certification is great for anyone's resume.

Self-paced training is available for those who want to train around their busy schedule, gain the same knowledge as the two-day course, and use the training as they work. There are several self-paced options designed for various business people, running diverse types of businesses.

For anyone who wants to make an upgrade in their business skills for the company they work for or to increase their hiring desirability, the training courses plus certification are worthwhile. If you just want to have someone walk you through how to use the program, then going to the class or going with a self-paced option is the way to learn what you need and get your questions answered.

Now that you understand the features available to you via QuickBooks support, it is time to go back to the plans and pricing and decide whether you want to add customer support options, go with a training program, or muddle through on your own. Remember, most of the online, monthly payment options have full customer support as part of the package, and thus may be worth the extra cost, plus the added features you gain over the one-time fee for the download version.

CHAPTER 5

SETTING UP QUICKBOOKS

QuickBooks is a simple install on your computer, if you decided to go with the desktop version. If you are using the online product, you won't need to install anything. However, you are going to set up the program with your business details, register your copy of QuickBooks, and start entering data, no matter the program choice you made.

QuickBooks Set Up for a New Business

Individuals who have a new business and use QuickBooks from the start have an easier time with the set up. There are fewer things to input at the beginning. You are working on the details such as vendors, suppliers, distributors, employees, and probably have one bank account for the business. Business owners who download the program after running their company for years have to "switch" over to QuickBooks, entering current data, but also everything that is relevant. It is the same if someone buys the business and will keep many of the vendors, employees, and other business concepts the business already has and adds QuickBooks.

QuickBooks will walk you through the set up. There are prompts for when and what information to enter. The basic steps are below and may change based on the version you are using.

1. Create a Username and Password (required at time of purchase or when you install the desktop version)
2. Set up company information (business name, address, email, website, Tax ID).
3. On the right side of the screen, go to your company name and click on it. This opens the account information. It shows your company details and allows you to upload your company logo. It will show up on your invoices, and other official documents.
4. Save the changes.
5. Add contact information including company phone.
6. In the address area, you can show your shipping and billing address. If they are the same you can mark that in this area, so your bills indicate where a company or person should send payment. Save the changes.

207

You are ready to start using QuickBooks.

Business Set Up when Adding QuickBooks

If you decided you needed accounting software after your business has been running for years, the set up will vary slightly.

1. Check to make sure the latest QuickBooks version will run on your computer. Older computers, such as anything previous to Windows 7 operating system, are no longer supported with updates or with most software programs.

2. If you are using an online version, you need to make sure your web browser can support the online login requirements, again, older systems may not be supported by the browser.

3. Follow the "set up" steps for a new business ensuring to input company name, address, phone, email address, website, and Tax ID number.

QuickBooks works for billing, receiving, Point of Sale, and payroll. More information needs to be added to use the aspects of the program you are paying for, such as payroll.

Vendors Set Up

Setting up vendors in QuickBooks is essential for paying bills. You can pre-populate vendor information in QuickBooks and keep track of expenses by vendor. It helps you create reports to see who you are spending the most money with, which is important for business health.

You can set up vendors manually, use an Excel file, or CSV file. If you are not computer savvy, it is better to have a local computer technician or QuickBooks walk you through how to import with excel or a .CSV file. If you have 10 vendors or fewer than adding them manually is an acceptable option. Uploading a .CSV file is the quickest method when you have the information electronically available and the understanding for how to import. (Note: some companies may be so old-school that manual entry is the only option even for thirty plus vendors. It is time consuming but worth every minute).

1. Sign in to your account, via desktop or online.
2. Go to the "Vendors" tab on the left-hand side of your screen.
3. Click on "New Vendor" on the right side of the screen.
4. Enter company name
5. Enter address, it should be the billing address.
6. Enter email, phone, website

7. If you know it, enter the billing rate, terms, any opening balance you have.

8. Add the account number you have with the vendor and their Tax ID.

There is a place to add billing and shipping addresses for all vendors. For instance, if the billing address is different to an address you would use for returns, you can make this clear when you add a vendor.

Any company that is not a corporation requires a 1099 form. You will want to mark the "track payments for 1099" for any company you spend over $600 with to ensure you are fulfilling your tax requirements.

Save the Vendor if you have finished completing the fields. There is an option of uploading attachments for specific vendors. For example, if there is any paperwork for the company you want to keep, you can add an attached file.

Once you are done with the first vendor, save, close that vendor, and start adding a new one. You can always go back into the Vendor area, click on a company, and edit the information. You can mark vendors who are inactive but keep the records of the company should you wish to use them again.

Add all the vendors you currently work with and, when this is done, move on to a new category, such as Employees.

Setting Up Employees for Payroll

Before you can pay your employees using the Payroll function, you need to add them to your QuickBooks program. You also want to understand the tax information you need to set up or have an accountant on hand to help you. Further details about creating paychecks will come later; however, it needs to be mentioned that you can gain help with payroll by paying for an added QuickBooks payroll service. The reasons for using an added service are discussed later.

Find the Employees Section:

1. Click on "Employees" in the left side menu.
2. Click "Add" employee.
3. The first screen is personal information, including legal name, address, and phone.
4. You need to enter the frequency of payroll, such as full-time, regular, part-time, or other options.
5. You will also add information from the W-4 form regarding withholding.
6. If your state has an employment tax, you will need to set it up based on your state requirements.
7. Enter the birthdate and hire date of your employees.

Once you have the employee details added under all tabs, including the withholding information for the employee, you can add a new employee. Continue the process until all employees are entered. You also have an option of adding part-time employees who may be inactive. You can mark them as inactive or active, as their status changes.

The "Employee" area is just to set up specific withholding information for the employee. To use Payroll, you need to set up the Payroll Taxes in a separate area, where the Federal and State taxes are automatically calculated. If you do not know this information, you will need an accountant to help you set it up.

Entering Payroll Taxes

You can manually create Payroll each time you pay an employee. We will discuss this later. However, if you want to make life easy and avoid missing any tax payments for Payroll, you should opt-in for the Payroll option with QuickBooks. Depending on your plan, it may require an extra fee, or you may be able to set it up and start using it right away. This section is solely the steps to get the correct taxes entered for what you will need to pay and how to calculate the deductions for your employees.

First, when you enter withholding information under each employee, you are one step closer to getting the Payroll taxes set up. The following are steps you will go through once you get into the navigation center under "taxes." You will go into the Payroll Tax Center and begin filling in the information to ensure you are in compliance.

1. Enter your business information into the Payroll taxes setup.
2. Add your FEIN
3. Using 941 or 944 Form for taxes, open the form and provide the information.
4. Set up the Payment/Deposit schedule for federal tax payments.
5. Enter your bank account and routing numbers
6. Use your online USER ID and Password for your bank to make the payments.

You are now set up to use QuickBooks for Payroll.

Tying Your Bank Accounts to QuickBooks

There are a few reasons you might want to have your bank accounts tied to QuickBooks. The first is to ensure you make payments and keep records as accurate as possible. QuickBooks enables you to reconcile your bank statement by importing the information and checking it against what you have entered as you paid bills and employees. You can set up more than one business bank account, if necessary. You might have two accounts, such as one you pay bills with and one you pay employees with, which means you need to check the correct account is assigned to the payments being made as you do them. You want to have a bank account tied to QuickBooks for supplies, like ordering more checks.

Typically, you set up one account first and then request QuickBooks to help you set up the second account, when you are ordering checks for those accounts. However, you can set up as many accounts as you want by creating two or more check registers.

1. Go to Chart of Accounts.
2. Type Ctrl N on the keyboard to open a new window.
3. Click "Bank."
4. Follow the on-screen prompts to enter the bank related information, including routing number and bank account number.
5. Save.

When you set up your bank accounts for QuickBooks, you will need to enter a "starting" balance. This information is to tell the program how much money is in the bank account right now, so when you reconcile the bank account later, the numbers will match. If you need to, you can adjust the balance during the reconciliation process to indicate the correct details. You do not have to add every bank account you have, but if you are going to use them for business reasons or if you are going to reimburse your personal account for a business expense, it is best to tie everything you can together in QuickBooks. It is easier in the long run than adding things later. But, of course, you can always add more details later.

You have completed the set up for QuickBooks. It is time to move on to more in-depth areas of QuickBooks to ensure you are using everything available to you in the accounting software. The arrangement of topics is in keeping with daily, occasional, and housekeeping tasks.

CHAPTER 6

BASIC STEPS TO OPERATING QUICKBOOKS - PART 1

Your focus, if you are going to hire an accountant or have one, is to use QuickBooks for bookkeeping. You want to understand the basic operations and then graduate to more in-depth topics. You will want to understand bookkeeping such as recording revenue, expenses, accounts payable and accounts receivable. Your ultimate goal is to run a functioning business at a profit, which takes employees, reports, and understanding of the company's bottom line. The basic steps for using and operating QuickBooks will help you do the aforementioned concepts.

Bookkeeping in QuickBooks

Snail mail is still a thing although many companies are going "paperless" by sending invoices and credit memos through email. However, the "tax man" has not changed their requirements. Businesses are required to keep their business files, including all details about expenses, accounts payables, accounts receivables, and payroll, on hand for seven years. You still need hard copies, in the event a computer dies, the backups disappear, and any number of things happen. It also makes good sense to have a hard copy, plus electronic versions of everything.

The point being made—you are going to record everything from the mail or email that is business related to your company's health. Bookkeeping is all about the data, which needs to be in the computer and in your files.

The basic steps to operating QuickBooks are all about the daily tasks you want to perform. It begins by creating invoices that are going to help you bring in the revenue.

Creating Invoices

Part of your task if you sell goods or services is to invoice companies or customers. We are not going to discuss what your business might do but give you the tools to help you. If you do not create many invoices, then this section is of little importance to you. But it is also worth knowing it exists.

You have done the preliminary work by setting up the vendors and customers you have.

Know the type of invoice you are creating, including product, service or professional.

1. Go to Customers
2. Select Create Invoices
3. Select the Invoice form you need, such as professional, product, service, or credit memo.
4. Identify the person receiving the invoice from your "customer" list.
5. You can decide to assign a "class" which would track the income. Class is how you are categorizing the products or services you are invoicing for, which helps you keep track of your inventory or services rendered.
6. Enter a date for the invoice
7. Give the invoice a number to help you track it.
8. If necessary, you can adjust the "billing" and "shipping" addresses.
9. Depending on the size of your business, you may also assign Purchase Order (PO) numbers.
10. Specify the agreed upon payment terms, such as net 30 days.
11. Add in other details that may apply, including name of sale rep, shipping date, shipping method, and whether it is FOB (free on board).
12. Make sure you enter a line for each item you are selling to this customer.
13. Specify any specific information or items

14. You can add a customer message.
15. Enter the sales tax
16. Print the invoice for packing and your files.
17. Save the invoice by clicking on "Save" you can save and create a new invoice or save and close out of the invoices if you are done for the moment.

You have the option of going in and correcting errors you make on invoices. We will look at that information later in troubleshooting tips. What you want to get used to is following the prompts. The information being asked is self-explanatory and something you should be used to providing on an invoice if you have been in any management, bookkeeping, or business-ownership position before.

The difference is using QuickBooks instead of Excel or handwriting the information. It keeps your communications professional, supplies clear terms, and helps the company or customer receiving the goods check everything is in the box or boxes.

Invoices also help you know exactly what money is outstanding and needs to be paid. Back in the explanation for why you want to use accounting software, it was discussed that QuickBooks enables you to complete daily tasks such as entering information and occasional tasks like tracking down money you are owed and re-invoicing if necessary.

By using the basic functions of QuickBooks, you can check the incoming payments to determine if you received the money you should have based on the payment terms provided to your vendors or customers.

Accounts receivable is just one section of your company that needs daily input. Your accounts payable should be tracked to help you make your payments on time.

Credit Memos

Your customers may have items "on account" such as goods they have not paid for because the terms are net 30 days or more. There are also times when your customer may need to send items back. Perhaps, the item was faulty, so they are returning it. Let's look at sending items back. We will use a bookstore example. When you send hardcover books back to the publisher or distributor because the softcover of a book comes out, it can create a cycle of new books and credit memos.

Issuing a credit memo to your customer helps you record the revenue you make accurately against deductions made to accounts. You want to know you are getting the correct amount of money from the customer, so you must record credit memos as much as you create invoices and record payments.

From the Customer menu:

1. Choose "Create credit memo/refund.
2. Identify the customer.
3. Add a date, number, and confirm you have the correct customer details.
4. Add a reason for the memo.
5. Save and Close or you can create a new memo.

The process helps you allocate credits you are giving to a customer when you are in the payment information. It is two-fold. The first step is making sure you notify the customer they have received a credit on their account, and you will adjust the amount owed on your end. The second step is to help the customer and you keep track of the actual amount due based on the terms of the invoice and any credits they received before payment was due.

Recording Revenue

Paying the bills and sending out invoices to make sure you get paid is part of any business. Another part of basic accounting is to keep up with outstanding payments you need to receive. Each time a check or credit card payment is made for an invoice, you want to keep track of that money. Your software needs to know money is coming in to ensure you are balanced with your bank statement. Part of your bookkeeper's job, or yours, is to record the revenue. Recording the revenue or payments is part of the accounts receivable function of accounting. It is also part of the daily tasks you perform, whether you sell goods or services. You might not deposit the money each day; however, you do reconcile your sales for services or goods each night.

What are the types of revenue?

- Payment for goods or services sold.
- Credit card charges.
- Cash earned in the point of sale system.

If you are a retail store, you will have credit card and cash earnings to record. You may also invoice for products you ship. For example, if you run a bookstore, you might ship books to a client out of town, invoice them, and receive a check in the mail. You might also have a library buy books from you on account and then you receive payment for those books later.

A service business may invoice for their services, such as coming by to fix the plumbing and giving the client a week to pay for those services.

If you distribute goods, such as being a publisher who sells books to a retail location, you invoice the bookstores and record the payments they make against their account balance.

The steps to record revenue, when it is a direct sale, are simple:

1. Under "Customer" choose "Enter Sales Receipt."
2. Identify who sent the payment.
3. Specify the reason for the receipt.

4. Provide a date.
5. Record the check number for the payment.
6. Enter the payment method.
7. Describe what was sold.
8. Enter sales tax.
9. Print receipt.
10. Save the sales receipt.

This type of record of inventory is if you are selling a product directly to the customer and need a receipt while they are in the store. You also have the choice of recording customer payments against invoices.

Customer Payments

Use this choice if you are logging revenue paid from invoices. You already understand how an invoice is entered. Now, you want to make sure you have the payment recorded against the invoice. A few things can happen. The customer may decide to pay only a partial amount on the invoice. The customer may pay the full amount. The client may also forget to pay on time, which is when you would need to send a reminder invoice. You can always go into invoices and print a new document to mail, you can edit invoices too, as a way to reflect the past due information.

The steps below are designed for a full or partial payment.

1. Under "Customers"
2. Choose "Receive Payments"
3. Find the customer who paid.
4. Specify the date the payment was made (if payment was made that day, record the date, if you are going through a backlog of bookkeeping use the date on the check or payment form.)
5. Enter the amount being paid.
6. You can also go into the "Pmt," drop down menu to choose the type of method used for the payment, such as check, credit card, or cash.
7. Enter the check number, if there is one.
8. You have the option of adding a memo.
9. At this point, you can also apply outstanding "credit" to the account, such as a credit memo you have yet to allocate to the customer.
10. Find the invoices the customer is paying for, to allocate those to the account.
11. If necessary, you can adjust for early payment or discounts not shown on the invoice.
12. Click Done
13. Click to "Record" the payment information by selecting "save and new" or "save and close."

Notice there is a place to assign a credit memo should a company, client, or customer be due money for returned or faulty items. You have already learned how to create a credit memo, and step 9 showed you how to apply the credit memo when you are recording the revenue (payment) the client sent.

Keeping on Top of Revenue Flow

You are running a business. You need to have a good inflow of money to keep going. When your customers are late with payments, it makes it difficult to continue running your business. There are ways to keep on top of your clients to ensure the money flows in and cutting off customers when they are showing they are unable to keep up with the payments owed.

QuickBooks has invoice reminders for you and your customers. If you use the online version, you would follow this procedure.

1. Gear Icon
2. Settings
3. Company Settings
4. Sales
5. Reminders
6. You can customize the reminder.
7. To send the reminder, go to the money bar and click on "Overdue."
8. Go to the client.
9. Find the action column, and from the drop-down menu, choose to send a reminder, and how you want to send it.
10. You can also create a "batch" action to send each client reminders of overdue payments.

Under the filter option on the left of the customer list, you can use the drop-down menu to select batch actions and choose an action to take.

You have the option of emailing, printing, or sharing invoice to send as a reminder.

In the online version, you will always see the money bar on the homepage. When you open it, you see open invoices, overdue, and payments made. You want to make certain you close an invoice as paid when you get payment. If you fail to do this, it may look like you have an outstanding balance, when you really do not.

When you know there are outstanding balances, it is important for you to create terms a client will want to stick to for making payments on time. You might implement such things as finance charges, which shows the client you are going to start charging interest if the money is not paid quickly. You can also set up "fees" that are not interest charges, but overdue payment fees that will make the client want to pay quicker. It is best that you develop a strict collection procedure with your clients.

The above is information for basic steps in recording revenues and assigning payments made to your company. You also have information with regards to keeping the money flowing in from customers. Part of basic operations in QuickBooks also includes recording expenses and paying the bills. We will assess those steps in part 2.

CHAPTER 7

BASIC STEPS TO OPERATING QUICKBOOKS – PART 2

Accounts Receivable is just a portion of the bookkeeping and accounting procedures you do daily. You also perform accounts payable functions, which can be split into two categories: recording expenses and bill paying.

Recording Expenses

Expenses for many companies are considered a different type of expenditure than accounts payable. Accounts payable is the term applied to short-term debt or money owed to your suppliers and creditors. For example, the liabilities you have such as vehicle loans, commercial loans, vendor and distributor payments to your suppliers and other revolving liabilities are under accounts payable.

Expenses are office supplies, energy bills, water bills and other utilities. Expenses can be things you pay for out of your personal pocket and reimburse yourself with, such as using paid outs or bill pay to write you a check for the amount spent.

Both types of business expenditures need to be recorded and allocated to an appropriate class or category. For example, you would label office supplies under the category office supplies, but include only things like paper, ink, pens, staples, and other simple items. Equipment such as new computers would be considered assets and not "supplies."

For typical operating expenses, you will usually pay those bills right away, but you still need to record the payments. With supplier and other creditor expenses, you may record the bills, but wait until you perform weekly tasks to pay the actual bill.

You want to keep track of what you need to pay and the terms behind those payments. Let's use an example. You are a distributor of a product. You import products from several manufacturers and then distribute them to your customers, who are vendors selling to multiple retail stores.

You pay for the products you import and bill customers for the products you distribute. In this scenario, you need to record each time you receive products by tracking the invoice number, payment terms, and whether you have paid the current invoice.

There are two choices you will make when it comes to bill paying. Are you going to pay now or later? You can always pay the invoice the minute you receive it, so you would record it and then set up to print the check for the invoice. You can also record the invoice, without paying it.

Paying a bill when it comes in is an excellent choice. You do everything at once and ensure nothing falls through the cracks. However, sometimes you need accounts receivable to be up-to-date to afford the large payments, which means you may need to wait to pay the bill, but you want to make sure you don't forget what you have to pay when.

Accounts payable method where you record the invoices and keep track of outstanding bills is often the most used method for businesses due to cash flow requirements.

Each step you want to perform is outlined below to help you record expenses and pay the bills.

Recording Bills

When you receive a bill, but are not ready to write the check, you want to record it.

1. Go to "Vendors."
2. Select "Enter Bills."
3. Choose the "vendor" the bill came from.
4. Enter the payment terms.
5. If you have a vendor reference number, you can enter it.
6. You can also record any memo for the bill, if necessary.
7. Go to the account column in the expenses tab and enter the expense account name.
8. Tab over to the amount column to enter the amount.
9. The items tab allows you to enter information about the bill, such as what you are paying for and how many you received.
10. Save the bill. You can "save and new" or if done "save and close."

Now that you have entered the bills, you have a record of what you are paying for or will pay for in the future. If you make a mistake, you can always delete the bill.

Go into the Accounts Payable register and select the bill you want to remove. Choose "edit" and then click "delete bill."

You also have the option of having QuickBooks remind you of the bills you need to pay. Go into Edit, Preferences, and click the "Reminders" icon which allows you to tell the program what you want reminders for, including paying bills.

The above information is about recording the bills as they come in, and not necessarily paying them. The next section will address further details about making payments.

Writing a Check

One method is paying bills by writing a check. Under this method, the invoice information ends up in the check register and happens simultaneously with creating checks. It is a slower method. Here are the steps:

1. Choose "Banking" from the menu.
2. Find "Write Checks" in the drop-down menu. (You can also click write checks in the banking section)

A screen will open, where you have a check format on the top and the expenses and items tabs in the middle of the screen.

3. Choose the bank account you will use to make the payment.
4. Fill in the date.
5. Put a name in the Pay to the Order Of section.

6. Enter an amount for the payment.
7. You can add the address and a memo to the check if necessary.
8. In the Account column assign an expense to associate with the payment.
9. In the Item section you can list what you purchased with the payment being made.
10. When done entering all the pertinent details, click save, either "new" or "close."

Close the window and get out of check writing if you only need to do one check. If you have multiple payments to make, click "Save and New" to keep writing checks.

When you have completed your data entry and are ready to print the checks, you will need to select the option to print. More information will be provided for how to print the checks. It is not included here because you may perform the check printing option weekly instead of daily.

Quick Accounts Payable

1. Go to "Banking"
2. Select "Use Register"
3. Fill in the details for the check, including payee name, account, and the amount. You can also

"split" the check to show it is for more than one expense.

4. When you are done entering the information click "record."

This method is mostly for expenses like the electricity bill. You can also use the slow method of writing a check for everyday business expenses. It is possible to write yourself a check as a way of reimbursing you for expenses you might have paid out of pocket or with your personal account. Under the quick accounts payable method, you have the option of transferring money from one business account to another should you need to reimburse an account for a payment made. As you can imagine there are plenty of things to learn about accounts payable methods.

Paying Bills Later

The reminder, you set up after you recorded the bills, tells you bills are in need of paying, so now you need to write the checks for the bills you entered.

1. From "Vendors" choose "Pay Bills."
2. Enter a Payment Date for the checks.
3. Set a date to show only the bills that need paying.
4. Use "sort" to help you sort the bills.
5. Identify which bills you intend on paying.

6. If necessary, such as to make a partial payment, change the amount.

7. Select the payment date, method, and bank account.

8. Select the "To be Printed" option to ensure you can print the checks.

9. Click "Pay Selected Bills."

Once you click pay selected bills they will be marked as paid and you can print the checks to mail. If something goes wrong with printing the checks, you can tell the system to print them again. It will give you easy to follow prompts to make sure everything worked out as it should with regards to printing checks and marking bills paid.

Printing Checks

1. Go to "File"
2. "Printer Setup"
3. Select "Check/Paycheck"
4. From the Printer Name list select the printer
5. Select the printer type if you need to.
6. Select the check style
7. Click printer setup if you need to change the font.
8. Click "OK" to finish.

You are now ready to start printing checks as you write them or later when you are paying bills.

If you are printing as you write the checks, you just need to click print in the "Write Checks" window.

If you are printing multiple checks, you will go to the register, mark the checks you want to print and then go to File, Print Forms, Checks, and print the checks you want.

The above information provides the basic details you need for recording your bills, paying the bills now or later, and how to print checks when you are ready to make the payments. You may perform the actual check printing once a week, but for those who want it as part of the daily tasks, you have the steps included with the daily tasks of entering bills and potentially making those payments.

Paying Electronically

Many companies, including energy companies, are making it possible to pay bills electronically instead of writing and printing checks. Whether you want to use a credit card to make the payments to reap the rewards of air miles or you want to use ACH payments, you can do so through QuickBooks.

Remember, when you set up the bank accounts? Well, you have imputed all the information you need to make a payment with your bank account. You just tie it with the company you are making the bill payment to and tell QuickBooks you made an electronic payment versus writing a check. As you create the bills to pay, you assign the payment type. It is as simple as following the prompts and associating the correct categories and payment type in the check register and accounts payable sections.

CHAPTER 8

BASIC STEPS TO OPERATING QUICKBOOKS – PART 3

Another part of operating your business is to ensure your bank accounts are reconciled. Balancing the checkbook requires you to perform functions like ensuring the checkbook details are up-to-date daily or weekly, and that you are recording the deposits, as much as you record the revenue and expenses. Deposits and QuickBooks are made when you actually take the money to the bank. You will also learn about using credit cards as part of your payment method of expenses you have in your company. The credit card information is separate from paying the bills because it is away for you to pay for goods or services on credit rather than a straight payment or supplier invoice.

Deposits in QuickBooks

The type of business you have will determine how much cash inflow you have and when you need to do deposits. The typical business has three deposits to record.

1. Cash sales
2. Credit Card sales
3. Invoice payments

Any retail company or hospitality industry will need to record their daily deposits. If the company also invoices their customers, such as invoicing a library for books bought from a bookstore, the money will be recorded as an invoice payment and needs to be deposited.

The bookkeeper has the responsibility daily, weekly, or monthly to record the incoming money and making sure the bank account tied to QuickBooks shows the deposits.

Making the deposits puts the money recorded from sales and customer payments as deposited instead of "un-deposited funds."

1. Go to "Banking."
2. Choose "Make Deposits."
3. Select the payments you are depositing.
4. Click "Ok."
5. Choose the Bank Account the deposits are going into.

6.   Choose the correct deposit date.

Click on "Save and Close" or make a new deposit.

Your checkbook details are now accurately showing the cash, checks, and credit card income you received.

Note that when you pay a bill and write the check, you update the checkbook details to reflect the outflow of money.

Business Credit Cards

Another area that you need to focus on is if you pay with credit cards for business expenses. The arrangement of credit card expenses as part of the checkbook details is due to tracking things like the funds that are going out as part of a "petty cash" option. Some companies keep petty cash on hand, while others simply use paid outs to take the money from the daily sales cash, and others track everything on credit cards. You know how to show an individual expense by paying a bill. You may still want to keep the expenses on a credit card as individual transactions. For example, if the card is used for fuel and meals, you may want to record the fuel as a separate expense for the month from the meals.

You can also decide that the "credit card" bill you pay is enough to show that there are expenses to record for the outflow of money. If you wish to tie a credit card to

QuickBooks as a means of using the credit card to pay for expenses and recording the information in QuickBooks, then you will want to set up a credit card account.

1. Go to "Chart of Accounts"
2. Click the Account Button on the screen and choose "New."
3. Select "Credit Card"
4. Put a name in for the account, such as who uses the card or the credit card company.
5. Type the card number into the Credit Card Account Number box.
6. Save and close.

The reason you may wish to do this as a way to keep your "checkbook" details is because you are actually able to enter each transaction you have made using the credit card. In fact, like the Check Register, you now have a Credit Card Register.

In Banking:

1. Select "Enter Credit Card Charges"
2. From the drop-down menu choose the credit card account
3. In the purchased from field enter the place you used the credit card.
4. Indicate if it was a purchase or credit.
5. Enter the date.
6. Type the amount.

7. If necessary, use a memo to add more information.
8. Fill in the expense's category.
9. Put the itemized breakdown of the information.
10. Record by hitting save and new or save and close.

If you need to, you can edit or void a credit card transaction you put in the register.

- Go to Chart of Accounts
- Find the credit card account
- Choose the transaction to delete, edit, or void.
- Save your changes.

Like the check register, you will eventually learn how to reconcile the accounts to ensure you and the company are matching for payments made on the account and charges made. As you saw in the instructions, you can record a payment you make to the credit card account instead of making it a purchase. The credit function lets you record the payments you made to the account; thus, you will balance with the statement when it comes in. Also, by recording the transaction in the check register and as a credit for payment made to the credit card, you will balance in both registers.

Other daily tasks include updating your inventory information, ordering more, and reconciling what you sold. However, before talking about inventory, you should understand the basic steps to payroll. While it is often a weekly, bi-weekly, or semi-monthly task, it is something you do frequently and is of highest importance to your employees. You need to know how to do this function immediately to keep your employees paid on time.

CHAPTER 9

PAYROLL EXPLAINED

Employees want their checks on the date promised. If you have hand-written checks or outsourced this procedure, you no longer need to do so because QuickBooks will do everything for you.

During the set-up phase, you learned how to enter employees into QuickBooks, assign their withholding details, and set up payroll taxes. Now, you are going to use the features by creating paychecks.

There are two ways to create paychecks. You can pay for the payroll service QuickBooks offers. It helps you automatically assign the tax information. It will also calculate each employee tax details to create the paycheck accordingly. QuickBooks has a manual payroll function, if you do not want to pay for the added service.

The one thing QuickBooks is not going to do is direct deposit. For direct deposit options, you need an accountant that has ADP or Paychex for their clients or sign up for those services.

If you want to use the online resource from QuickBooks be prepared to pay $200 or $500 per year. The basic service will help with the checks, but you still do the work of filing the payroll taxes. The more advanced version will help with payroll forms and checks.

For companies that have fewer than 15 employees, there is no reason to pay out the $200 per year or even more. Doing the payroll manually takes less than 30 minutes, even if you are imputing all the tax deductions for each check.

There are some steps that will help you ensure the right information is provided, such as entering all the withholding information and setting up the payroll schedule. If necessary, go back into each employee and make certain you have it set up for regular hours, and the payment periods you prefer, such as weekly, semi-monthly, or bi-weekly. You can also choose monthly.

1. On the screen, find the employees section or use the menus to open Employees and then "Pay Employees."
2. Check the pay period end date is correct.
3. Check the date that will be on the check is right.
4. Click on the employees who you are creating paychecks for, you might have some part-time

employees who are not being paid each time but are active.

5. Once all employees are check-marked, click "open paycheck details."

6. In this section, you can add hours, check the date range, and manually enter the tax information for this pay period. (You may need to do this if you have not paid for the QuickBooks service or set up the tax details for each employee).

7. After all paychecks are accurate with date, hours, and taxes, save and close.

8. Click "create paychecks."

9. Review the information.

10. Print the checks, there are a couple of steps to printing, so follow the prompts, and if something does not print correctly, you can tell it to reprint certain checks or all checks.

It is easier if you have the tax information set up in QuickBooks even if you are manually entering the employee hours or not using the online service. However, it is not the end of the world if you want to take more time to create paychecks, it does mean you will need to have an accountant help you with your tax liabilities regarding payroll.

Pay Tax Liabilities

If you have payroll set up with tax information, you can manually go into Employees, and Payroll Taxes and Liabilities.

From this section you will click the payroll liability you are paying and click "view/pay." It will create a check and put it in the register, you can also print the check.

Unless you pay for the payroll service, you are not going to find the quarterly and annual returns and wage statements are available to you. You may also have to calculate your tax liabilities outside the program.

These features are something you want to consider, weigh the costs of from an accountant standpoint, and determine if paying for QuickBooks basic or full service is worth the help provided.

The one thing you do not want to do is forget to make the Federal and State payments required for the payroll. Small companies often benefit from manually creating the checks in house but letting an accountant deal with the tax side of things.

QuickBooks and Employee Hours

The above discussion and how-to manually create paychecks, assumes your employees do not use the employee hour function in QuickBooks. Make sure you have the QuickBooks plan that includes time tracking.

Freelance or self-employed versions do not, but the Pro, and above software programs do.

1. Go to the Gear Icon on the Toolbar (in the online version)
2. Under Company, go to Account and Settings
3. Select "Advanced"
4. Go to "Time Tracking"
5. Set your preferences, such as timesheets or billable to a certain customer.
6. Select Save and close out.

You also need to add users for time tracking, so your employees can "punch in."

1. Since you are still in the Company area after you close the "advanced settings, go to Manage Users.
2. Select Add User
3. Select Time Tracking Only
4. Next
5. Select the employees to add
6. Save

You can decide to make the time billable, which would ensure you allocate the time spent on projects and jobs to a specific customer. This is helpful if you have a service business like a construction company and need to show the customer the hours worked.

You can also have the option of creating a report for time tracking, which would show the activities based on the employees so you can pay them for the time they worked. This function is under the "reports" menu in your QuickBooks program.

Your employees will need to go into the time tracker to sign on and off for work. Employees should login and access their weekly or bi-weekly timesheet.

1. Under Employees, you will go to Enter Time and create the timesheet based on your pay period.
2. Create one for each employee by going to their name in the drop-down menu.
3. Have the employee enter their hours each day.
4. Save and close.

When you are ready to do the payroll, you can then access the timesheets and have the hours appear in the create paycheck area. This helps you electronically record the hours worked, calculate the taxes to deduct, and then write the checks using QuickBooks. You will want to review the weekly timesheets, either by accessing the report or by looking at every person individually. As the person making the paychecks, you want to ensure your employees have entered the correct data before you make the paychecks. It becomes more complicated if someone forgets to add their hours appropriately.

You would have to enter the data for the next pay period but assign it correctly as regular income. You do have the function to add in overtime, vacation, and sick pay.

These options, if you supply them to your employees, would need to be noted under their employee profile and then as you enter their hours you would allocate everything appropriately.

Remember you have tutorials you can view online, if you need to discover more about payroll entering, including how to update employee information such as changes to vacation time, personal days, and overtime.

In the employee section, when you edit your employee information you can change their wages as you provide raises. You need to update any changes to their hours or wages, prior to creating the checks. If you do not remember to adjust the wagers or hours, you can do so manually, but you should remember to go in and make those adjustments before you create checks the next time.

CHAPTER 10

INVENTORY TASKS

For some companies, inventory is a part of the business. Even for companies that offer services, keeping track of inventory can be helpful. As an example, we will discuss an internet service provider. The ISP has routers, modems, connection wires, and may have wireless equipment for "access points" that project the Internet signal to multiple customers rather than operating on fiber optic wire. Such a company would need to keep track of the access point equipment and the internet equipment they rent or sell to the customer. While, the inventory might be small, compared to a bookstore that could have thousands of books, the business still needs to keep up with inventory.

You will need to track inventory, keep up with inventory as you purchase and sell items, use purchase orders to help track it, and adjust what you have in stock versus what it shows is in stock. If you have more than one business location, you may need to keep track of inventory for multiple locations.

Setting up Inventory

You need to tell QuickBooks you want to track inventory.

- Go to Edit
- Preferences
- Select "Items and Inventory"
- Check "Inventory and Purchase Orders" is active.
- You can also tell QuickBooks to warn you if you do not have enough inventory.

Next, you will need to create an item list. Any items you intend to have in your inventory need to be on this list. You should set up the initial list and as you buy new inventory, you can add new items as you create purchase orders. You will keep updating your item list to help you track the inventory. You have the option of deleting things you cannot get again or do not want, as well as adding new products that you wish to bring in to your store.

Buying Stuff and Inventory

Creating a PO when you make an order is the best way to update your inventory. However, there are times when you may buy things in person and pay for them at the time or receive a bill in the mail. It would mean there is no purchase order in the system.

Let's say you bought a few items at a show and you are being billed later.

1. Go to Vendors
2. Receive Items
3. Receive Inventory
4. Select Receive Inventory without a Bill
5. Fill in the information for the vendor, if it is a new vendor make sure you add them.
6. Click the "items" tab
7. In the columns begin adding information about the product
8. Add in the quantity and your costs
9. Click "save and new" or close if there is nothing else to add.

Since you received the items and created a PO, you can go into the vendors area, click on enter bills for received items, and ensure you make the payment to the company.

If you have the item and the bill, you can enter everything all at once.

You still go to vendors:

1. Click Receive Items and Enter Bill.
2. Fill out the information for the vendor.
3. Go to the Items tab and start adding the details.
4. Save the information and either create a new one or close out of the area.

There are also times when you need to record the stuff you sell. Your inventory is in a constant flux of adding new items and selling what you have. Anytime you make a sale and it is recorded in QuickBooks through the Point-of-Sale system or with a sales receipt, your inventory will adjust. You don't have to update your inventory record because you record the sale in some way to indicate the sale has occurred, and what type of tender was given for the sale.

Creating Purchase Orders

While on the discussion of inventory and receiving new items, it is a clever idea to consider how to create the purchase orders for those orders you make. The advantage of QuickBooks is you don't need to use Excel or Word to create a document to fax or email to the companies you order from—you can use QuickBooks purchase orders, and let the software do the work for you.

It is important to add any new vendor you may order from prior to creating a purchase order.

1. Go to Vendor
2. Click "Create Purchase Orders"
3. Choose the correct vendor from the list.
4. Choose the inventory items you want to order; you can do this through the "class" list.
5. You can also start typing the item name in the item column and things will appear for you to choose.
6. Enter the item and the quantity.
7. If you need to add a memo in the memo field.
8. Click print to get a copy
9. Click save and new or close out of the PO area when you are done.

You will have the option of choosing how you want to submit the order, whether you do so electronically or call it in.

As with any other task in QuickBooks there are ways to ensure you get reminders when you need them. You may forget about an order because it is a busy time of year and you can go back in to see if you have received against all PO's created and if not, you can start looking into what happened. The fact that you have reports and reminders that help you check on things, as well as the option of going into the PO and adding things a day or so later, ensures you keep on top of your company business.

For companies that have multiple locations, you are better off with setting up multiple companies with QuickBooks and telling the program which location you want to work with for orders and other data sets. It is not easy to have more than one location's inventory tracked, unless you set up item numbers based on locations or you have multiple company details set up for your business.

Remember, QuickBooks is not set up for large businesses with more than 50 employees or multiple locations selling inventory. It works for service-oriented companies because you pay employees, bring in revenue, but don't have to track inventory.

CHAPTER 11

BUDGETING

The three financial reports, income statement, statement of cash flows, and balance sheet are designed to help you correct issues with your company's operations and to help you budget for the next quarter or year. The financial reports offer insight into trends, which help you determine if you need to order supplies. Creating the budget is considered an occasional task because you may make changes as things happen throughout the year to reallocate funds from one area to cover another expense. It falls under the occasional tasks along with the discussion on printing checks and payroll. It is a task that will require housekeeping tasks before it can be performed.

Going back to our bookstore example for a moment, consider if it is the only store in town and in a tourist community. The main period of sales would be during the height of the tourist season. It would be correct to assume the shop orders more books for the increase in customers and fewer during the off season. But one also has to account for whether each year will see the same influx of tourists. If information shows a year on year increase for the last two years, the trend will likely continue, unless economic strains occur throughout the country or world. The black and white financial reports help someone assess past and current trends, while also helping in the decision-making process for whether to allocate funds to different departments.

The budget comes in when you decide if your company has areas of struggle or is in a good situation, and whether you want to improve business with more or less advertising, carrying fewer or more items, and ensuring you maintain your budget.

We will discuss another example. We will say a piece of equipment breaks down in the first quarter. The budget for that department has to use two quarters worth of their budget, which puts a strain on the next quarter. Using the budget and financial reports, a company can decide if changes should be made to other departments to cover the large and unforeseen expense.

Creating the budget is something you do each year at the beginning of the year. You also have the option of amending it each quarter. To set up a budget go to planning and budgeting in the company section.

Budget Steps

1. Click set up budget
2. Select the year you are budgeting.
3. Select the type of budget you want to establish. You have an option of creating an income and expense budget or a budget of year-end asset, liability, and equity balances. Once you input for a budget income statement amounts or balance sheet amounts, click next.
4. Provide the information requested by the software.
5. If you want to start a new budget or start with last year's numbers, you can. Make your choice and choose finish.
6. Start entering budget information for the departments you plan to allocate funds to and once you are done save the work.

You can go into the budget and adjust it as needed. QuickBooks allows you to forecast profits and losses, project cash flows, and plan for things that may come up for income or expenses.

It is up to you to decide what types of items will go into the budget. You may have advertising, office supplies, inventory, wages, taxes, and related categories listed on your budget.

Tips for Budgeting

- Assign each expense and income a class in QuickBooks. You want to make sure everything has a category for the type of expense it is.

- Each month you will have different expenses; however, the categories these expenses fall into need to fit the quarterly budget. For example, you may not have office supplies each month because you buy in bulk. Yet, you want to make certain you have a budget category set up and assigned an amount.

- List all debts the company has, including any loans that are currently in repayment. Certain debts may be paid each month, like the employee credit card.

- It is best to assess the budget on a quarterly basis to see where you may need to reassign funds or cut expenses. Do not be afraid to find deals on office supplies, cut back your employee's meals, and other areas when you have more important expenses to worry about.

- Your budget is meant to be a schedule of payments, which includes the invoice terms you are responsible for throughout the year.

- The previous years' need to help you create a buffer for a change in sales or services. In a business, you never know what may occur in terms of economic downturns or upturns. Your budget is meant to keep you on track to cover your costs and employee payments. You also have to project expenses like replacement vehicles, computers, and other equipment. It is possible to run on a deficit in one quarter and positive in another.

- The key is to ensure you are running in the black for the year, whether you have some months at a deficit.

If you are a freelancer or work on commissions, things will differ slightly. Freelancers may pay commissions to get outside work accomplished, but they rarely have employees. Your budget is usually dependent on the amount of work you do, with few assets.

Freelancers like writers, artists, and other services usually work from home. You can have a home-based service business, such as commercial kitchen equipment repair. You have few inventory items you use to replace parts, typically, you order the parts needed when you need them. Your job is contingent on something breaking down or needing its maintenance, as per the manufacturer's maintenance schedule. In situations like these, it is harder to budget on a quarterly basis. However, you should still have a plan for your company.

- Marketing and advertising expenses should increase when work is slow.

- Even if you are not being paid, you need to find ways to ensure you get more work coming your way.
- You have to sell yourself more.

A function of QuickBooks is to tie in with hosting a website. If you decide you want to add a package with hosting services, you can create an ecommerce or services website, and use social media tie-ins to prompt your company.

When work is slow, you need to work harder to market your skills, not only locally, but globally depending on what your skills are.

It becomes a budget more about time than incoming funds. However, you also need to realize what you make one month may need to carry you through a lean month or five. For this reason, keeping on top of the budget, correcting the forecasting for a better projection of income, and saving money when it matters is necessary.

Freelances may work their budget each month, which is fine and possible with QuickBooks. The added benefit of the online freelancer program is to have a software program geared more towards your potential income and help you budget more appropriately based on those monthly expenses you must pay.

If you are unsure what budget categories to use, consult an accountant. Your accountant will have what they call a "Chart of Accounts" which is how you allocate your income and expenses. The categories your accountant uses are based on the deductions your business can take. Meals and entertainment are consolidated into one category. Vehicle mileage is another category.

From the above tips and discussion, you should have a good understanding of budget topics, why budgeting is important, and how it differs for the freelance or commission style work.

CHAPTER 12

FINANCIAL REPORTING WITH QUICKBOOKS

Reports are usually part of the housekeeping tasks you are going to perform. The financial reports listed here are something you print for the budget, taxes, and to keep around for the government audits. There are more housekeeping tasks to discuss after you learn how to print the main three financial reports.

QuickBooks provides reports to help companies check on the business' health. Balance sheets, statement of cash flow, income statements, and other reports are available for you to print and check. How often you look at these reports is up to you. You should make them part of the occasional business you take care of as the bookkeeper/owner. The type of reports you want to print will also depend on the business you run. The steps to create these individual reports and others you might find useful are examined in this chapter. Remember, you have training and QuickBooks help to use should you find there are reports you need that are not listed in this section.

Before you print reports or decide they are imperative to your company's operations, you need to know what they are, why you need them, and then you can learn how to create them.

Balance Sheet

The balance sheet is a statement showing assets, capital, and liabilities. It is helpful to balance your income and expenditures for specific periods, such as quarterly health checks. If you want to know how the business is doing, what it made for the quarter, and how high your expenditures are to improve your company's health, a balance sheet is a place to start. You will gain information about your assets, what the company owes, and its overall net worth. The QuickBooks balance sheet is organized into two sections, so you can see what you have with what you owe subtracted. Together with the income statement and statement of cash flow, you can spot trends in your company, particularly, with customers paying you and whether you can pay your bills.

QUICKBOOKS

How to Create the Balance Sheet

First, you need to make a choice regarding the type of report you want for the Balance Sheet. The standard report will show the information we have discussed for a specific date. Detailed sheets add to the information for a month period with a beginning and ending balance for the specified month. A summary Balance Sheet has only the ending balances for all the accounts instead of each individual account. You can also create a year on year comparison or set a specific class for the report, such as assigning all the income and expenses to specific expense categories.

1. In the File menu, choose Reports.
2. Chose Company and Financial in the reports drop-down menu.
3. Chose the type of Balance Sheet.
4. Print it if you want or save it to your computer.

Statement of Cash Flow

The statement of cash flow will summarize the cash and assets that enter and leave the business. Combined with the balance sheet and income statement, businesses need to print these reports for the year. It was made a mandatory part of financial records in 1987. The cash flow statement helps a company see how it is running, where the money is coming from, and how much is spent. It is also a way to see how much cash is available for operating expenses and whether a company can pay its debts. The idea behind the cash flow statement is to help with investors or help creditors see the health of a company. The cash flow statement will typically show cash, accounts receivable, accounts payable, depreciation of equipment, and inventory. The cash flow statement uses information from the balance sheet and income statement to populate.

The statement made through QuickBooks will have six pieces of information:

- Operations
- Cash balance
- Finance
- Investing
- New cash balance
- Forecasting

You can create the statement with the direct or indirect method. The direct method will show in and out flows of money by subtracting the money spent from what was received. The indirect method begins with the net income and factors in things like depreciation.

1. From file or the left-side menu, select reports.
2. Find the statement of cash flows.
3. Select it to open it.
4. Customize the report for what you may need, such as putting in a date range for the report period.
5. Run report
6. Print the report, if necessary.

Income Statement

You can create different reports for income statements, like the profit and loss statement. If you want the full version of the income statement, go to the reports area in your version of the program and search for the statement you want. Some consider the profit and loss statement to be the income statement. Both are going to show the revenue and expenses for the period you choose to help you focus on your company's performance. There will usually be four items of information on the full report: expenses, revenue, gains, and losses. If you want to, you can just show the profit and loss, without the revenue and expenses, but with a net revenue provided.

The reason you want this statement is to show the net income, total revenue, and see if your company is performing correctly, managed right, or if there are areas that are underperforming.

1. Choose income statement from the search results.
2. Customize the statement for the dates, columns, notes, reason, and other items.
3. Run the report.
4. Save it to your computer and print it.

A Profit and Loss Statement

1. From reports, choose company and financial.
2. Choose profit and loss standard.
3. You can modify the report to show up to 12 months of data.
4. You can also select total only or month.
5. Ok
6. Print, if you need to.

CHAPTER 13

BALANCING THE CHECK REGISTER

Daily tasks are about recording information. Occasional tasks keep you on point for ensuring payments are made, reminders are sent, and you are on budget. Housekeeping tasks are often drudgery. You don't want to do them, but you need to, and they are where it matters if you are a good bookkeeper. If you are sloppy in your work, leaving bills to be entered, invoices have paid, and lack the task management to enter all data as it comes in, then balancing your check register is difficult.

It should be easy. Balancing the check register is actually so simple compared to the old method of manually checking your written register against the bank statement, you shouldn't fear it. If you maintain your records correctly, you will not have to explain the differences between the two accounts, unless it has to do with checks you wrote, but they did not clear before the bank statement.

The Steps for Balancing

1. Under Banking, select reconcile
2. Choose the bank account.
3. Put in the statement date
4. Verify the opening balance
5. Enter the ending balance from your bank statement
6. Enter any bank fees, plus the date
7. Enter any interest income, if any and the date it occurred
8. Continue

The first thing you want to do is mark any deposits that cleared. If you see a deposit on the statement that is not in QuickBooks, it means you did not enter the record of the deposit. You should record it now.

Make sure you mark each deposit that has cleared and entered any that you did not do prior to balancing the check register. Once you have marked all deposits, it is time to find all the checks that cleared.

9. Find the first check that has cleared and mark it as such.

10. Record any check you see on your bank statement, but that did not show up in the check register for QuickBooks.

11. Continue with these steps until you have all the checks from your bank statement marked as cleared and entered in QuickBooks.

At this point, you should see a difference between the cleared balance and ending balance as zero. However, if there are things you missed or accidentally selected, you may see a balance that is different than zero. You would need to go back through to find the error. You can also click reconcile now and it will show you a box opening the adjustment window.

In that window you can attempt to find the error or enter an adjustment to reconcile. Once you are done, return to reconcile. For those who show zero, just reconcile the account and you are done.

There are some typical reasons you might not reconcile between your bank statement and QuickBooks.

- You have a transaction the bank has not processed yet, but you select it as cleared.
- You did not enter something the bank statement has or forgot to select clear.
- A reversed transaction occurred, whether by design or accident, and now you need to correct the issue or wait for the bank to show the correction.

- You have a transaction that was partially made, and you forgot to go in and reflect the partial payment or the full payment when it happened.
- You might have transposed numbers.
- You definitely want to look for anything that matches the exact amount you are off, but do not forget it could be more than one transaction error.
- You can click "locate discrepancies" to help you.
- Have a second person checking your work.
- Leave it for this month and try to reconcile correctly next month. You might find a transaction you thought cleared and did not.

The beauty of being linked with your bank accounts are that you can reconcile with online statements. You can import your statement from your bank during the reconciliation of the check register, which allows it to automatically find the transactions by amount, check number, and other information.

It works by automatically assigning bank statement information to what is shown in your check register. At the end of the process, it will tell you if there are items not in the check register, but on the bank statement. At this point, you get a chance to add them to your QuickBooks program, so that you reconcile perfectly.

The process described in the chapter is primarily for those who do not import their bank statements but do things in a non-online capacity.

For those who keep up with entering payments, deposits, and other revenue daily or weekly, it should take a couple minutes to reconcile the check register and move on.

CHAPTER 14

REPORTS

As part of the occasional tasks, you may want to run a variety of reports to check on your business' performance. There are numerous reports QuickBooks provides. All it takes is knowing what each report is, how it can help you, and how to print it. We have already talked about the three main financial reports, but there are more options like sales tax and other tax reports. The following is a list of the reports you can access in QuickBooks.

- Customers and Receivables – reports designed to help you track customer invoices. The report can list unpaid invoices, organize them by customer, job, or length of time it is outstanding.
- Sales – reports that show you who your customers are and what you have sold. The sales reports can be broken down by item, sales rep, and customer.

- Time and Mileage – for each job you have, you can run a report for the time spent on the job and any vehicle mileage required to complete the job. Under these reports you get to see the profitability, estimate comparison to actual costs, time and functions completed, and vehicle mileage.

- Purchases – designed to show who, what, and how regarding items you purchased for the store. You are able to customize the reports by vendor or item. You also have purchase order reports that show any outstanding orders to help you track what has arrived and what is still incoming.

- Inventory – as with purchase orders, you can use this report to track what you have on hand, what you sell the most of, and then design a new purchase order based on what your business needs to order.

- Vendors and Payables – the account payable reports are designed to help you pay your bills. The report can list everything by vendor or oldest unpaid first. There is also a report for sales tax liability generated once you know what is paid or unpaid.

- Employees and Payroll – tracking what your employees are doing, what you have paid for, and therefore your tax liability is imperative, so the three reports for employees and payroll are essential to your company's operations.

- Accountant and Taxes – like other tax liabilities, you need to track tax reports, general ledger reports, journal reports, and trial balance information, which the accountant and taxes reports help you do.

- Banking – if you ever need a bank statement based on QuickBooks, it can be found in the banking reports.

- Budget and Forecasts – how do you know your quarter or year was on target or where the breakdown occurred? The reports that print the budget, your forecasts, and assess whether you are on target.

- List – report lists will show contacts, customer, vendor, and other name-oriented lists, which can help with inventory particulars.

- Industry Specific – depending on your version of QuickBooks you may have reports that are helpful to your business type. Some QuickBooks versions have reports for accountants, manufacturers, contractors, wholesalers, retailers, nonprofits, and professional service firms.

- Contributed Reports – provides access to custom report templates from Intuit and other companies that may help you generate reports you require for your business.

- Custom – Like contributed reports, custom options help you customize summary and transaction reports.

Knowing the reports are available in QuickBooks is just the beginning. Creating the report and printing it is essential.

Creating Reports

All the reports will be housed in the "reports" menu. In the drop-down menu, you will need to select the report you want. When it opens to the report options screen, there are ways to customize the report to fit the dates and information you want from it.

Click the "ok" option to get the report to generate. It will appear on screen. If you do not want to print, you can use your arrow keys to move up and down. It allows you to view the various parts of the report on screen.

For those who want to print the report, click on the print icon at the top of the report. The print dialogue box will appear and from there you can choose the correct printer, and then print the report.

There are other benefits to creating the reports, such as exporting the report into an Excel or .CSV file. Sometimes, reports are set up to best-fit all QuickBooks users, which might include information you do not want.

By exporting to a file, you are able to edit and rearrange the report.

QuickBooks does provide options in the program to edit and rearrange some of the information. For example, you can click on customize report, share template, comment, memorize, email, Excel, and more. If you have more than one person in the company who will use the report, then sharing it is a helpful option. Memorize is also a way to share a report to a group.

Sometimes you need to turn on functions in QuickBooks to make use of a report. Job information is one of those functions.

Job Estimating, Billing, and Tracking

Before you can generate reports and monitor how jobs are going, you must turn on those functions in the program.

1. In Edit, select Preferences
2. Click Jobs and Estimates
3. Go to Company Preferences Tab
4. Select Yes to tell it you want to create estimates and progress invoices

Progress invoices are those you provide to the customer to gain money during an ongoing job. For example, you may receive an amount of money upfront for materials to build a house. A month later, you might bill another chunk of money for the progress you made, and at the end you settle up what is left.

Once you have the functions in place, you need to understand how you set up the job, create the estimates, and track the billing information.

Job: The Set Up

To track the invoices and costs, you need to set the job up in QuickBooks. In fact, before you can create an estimate, you need to tell the system you have a new potential job.

- Under Customers, go to Customer Center
- Enter a new customer or choose one from the list
- Add job
- Enter the details of the new job

With the set up complete, you are ready to create the job estimate.

- In Customers, select Create Estimates
- Fill in the blanks for the job form, which is in the drop-down list.
- Add as many details as required
- Save and close it.

You can come back to the estimate when you learn more information about the job. For example, you might not have the cost of an item needed for the work. If you have a construction company and are estimating the cost to build a house, you might need to research a couple of windows, flooring, cabinet, and other companies. You may also be waiting for estimates from sub-contractors on things like concrete, foundation work, plumbing, and electric. You are always able to go into the customer job file and revise the estimate.

Once you have submitted the estimate to your customer and it has been approved, you can go into QuickBooks and turn the estimate into the invoice. If there are any changes you and the customer agreed to make now is the time to edit the estimate one final time before you complete the steps to turn it into an invoice.

1. In the Customer Center, find the customer and open the screen.
2. A list of estimates appears, click on the one you want to work with.
3. Click the "Create Invoice" option.
4. You still have a last chance to make modifications.
5. Save and close or go to a new estimate.

As with any job where you are estimating the cost of the time, work, and products, there are times when the estimate and the actual cost may differ. QuickBooks allows you to compare the estimated and actual costs to show your customer why you might need to charge a little more or where you were able to help save them money. This ties back to the reports we discussed above about jobs.

When the amounts differ from the estimate and actual, you want to charge everything appropriately and in a way that looks professional. Open customers and create invoices. Find the correct customer.

When the screen opens, you are able to click on add time and costs. You will be able to enter the billable time and costs the job has and if necessary, you can add a markup. As you complete the changes, click okay and then save and close.

Under jobs in the time and mileage reports, you track the costs and are also able to print the reports, as mentioned earlier, to help you show the customer what is happening with their job.

Reports are your friend. When you walk into a bank for a construction loan to build spec houses, remodel homes for resale, or any number of reasons your specific business may have, reports will show how healthy your company is.

You benefit from the information because you can also see where you may need to make changes in employees, costs, and other business-related expenses. Some reports may be helpful for your accountant, but many of them are for you to interpret.

QUICKBOOKS

CHAPTER 15

HOW TO USE QUICKBOOKS EFFICIENTLY

Adding QuickBooks to your business can save you a lot of time. It can help you determine the health of your company, but you do want to use it in the most effective way. Whatever is going to save you time and allow your focus to be on bringing in more revenue is worth it. But how worth it is up to you. As you learned in payroll, you can do everything manually and take thirty minutes to an hour creating paychecks. You can also pay $200 per month to make it easier. It is possible to have an accountant come, set it up for the tax information, and ensure creating paychecks is simpler. The decisions are up to you; however, this guide can give you the "why" for whether you want to change current procedures or keep some of the old concepts.

In a discussion of efficiency, it should be noted that technology can fail us. If a storm knocks out the power, you are now back in the pre-tech days where everything was done by hand. A bit ago someone told a co-worker about a shop that got rid of its old knuckle cruncher—a credit card machine—using carbon paper to record numbers. The old-fashioned device was called "obsolete" and not worth keeping. For those who think about technology failing, it seems silly to call it obsolete. But, consider the majority of credit cards today—many are no longer embossed—meaning the numbers are not raised, so the machine cannot record the numbers on the carbon paper. For those cards, such a machine is obsolete, but for the embossed cards—it still works.

You want to think about efficiency in your company, but don't go too far in the other direction. If someone has a gift certificate for your store and the computer POS system is not working due to a power outage—it is great if you can go to a hard copy of those gift certificates to record the information until you can enter it in the POS system.

Hire an Accountant

Hiring an accountant is worthwhile depending on how many employees you have, the job duties required, and your knowledge. Not everyone is an accountant. Some of the simple things are easy to understand, but you are not going to research the tax law changes that happen each year. You are not going to have time, as a business owner, to keep up with certain accounting procedures.

There are several reasons to have an accountant. The best part is you can pay your accountant for the work they do, without hiring a full-time person, in your small business. Larger small businesses may have the budget for an accountant/bookkeeper and that is worthwhile, if you can afford the person.

Hire a Bookkeeper

Some businesses have an accountant they use for the important projects, such as payroll taxes, Federal and State taxes in April. You can also hire a bookkeeper to come in to conduct occasional and housekeeping tasks. The person would enter information, print reports, and file for you. They could also create paychecks.

If you have a person on staff that is a manager or who has worked with QuickBooks in a management capacity, you could assign bookkeeper duties to that person.

By hiring an accountant or bookkeeper, or one person to fill both shoes, you are freed up to do more important business concepts. It ensures you are using QuickBooks efficiently because you are using your people effectively.

Shortcuts for QuickBooks

There are plenty of things you can do in two or more ways with QuickBooks, such as using the upper toolbar to find the drop-down menus, using the side menu display, or the main panel that says, company, reports, and employees. The cheats in this section are ways to use the keyboard to access or perform certain QuickBooks functions. If you are a mouse lover, then these may convert you to using the keyboard, since it can be a time-saving factor.

- To save a transaction: ALT S
- Save and move to new: ALT N
- Open the chart of accounts: CTRL A
- Copying items: CTRL C
- Deleting items like a check: CTRL D
- Editing register info: CTRL E
- Display search window: CTRL F
- Opening Create Invoice: CTRL I
- Create New: CTRL N
- To print: CTRL P
- To create and display a quick report: CTRL Q
- TO open the register window: CTRL R
- Pasting copied items: CTRL V
- To write checks: CTRL W
- Undo: CTRL Z
- Save Changes: CTRL Enter

- Inserting a new line: CTRL Insert
- To close a window or QuickBooks: ESC

These are just a few of the quicker ways you can perform actions in QuickBooks using your keyboard, rather than the mouse.

CHAPTER 16

HELPFUL SELF-EMPLOYED TAX DEDUCTIONS FOR SMALL BUSINESSES

Owning a small business makes you want to save as much money on expenses as possible. It can be hard because many of the deductions for taxes are disappearing. Thankfully, things change, so what you may not like in the coming years regarding tax deductions could change after another few years. As you struggle with finding deductions or realizing some things are not worth tracking anymore due to tax law changes, keep in mind the following information. Mileage, meals, and home-based deductions are still worthwhile for now. Your accountant can help you or your use of TurboTax through Intuit. QuickBooks can pair with TurboTax to help you maintain the proper tax filings, even without an accountant, at least if you are a self-employed person with few employees or working out of your home.

You do not want to miss the benefits provided, given how small they are.

Mileage Tax Deduction

Mileage is still one of the biggest deductions you can take on your IRS filings. In 2018, it was announced there would be a "standard mileage rate." This rate works for businesses, medical reasons, and in support of charitable organizations. For businesses, you can deduct 54.5 cents per mile for the miles you drive relating to business.

For example, if you drive 50 miles to meet a new client or pick up office supplies, you can deduct 54.5 cents per mile, totaling up to $27.5.

Anytime you go somewhere for business you need to record how many miles you traveled. Even if you only go one mile per day, it can add up for the entire year. Now, going from home to your office does not count, but any trip to a store, to a job, or other related business mileage can be counted.

Note: you can deduct vehicle mileage if you use your personal vehicle for business. It is imperative you record all mileage usage, including the personal details to show what is and is not related to business. Even if you do errands that are business and personal, make clear distinctions between each stop. If you are ever audited, you will need to show your documentation.

Meals Tax Deduction

There are reasons you may go out to eat and consider it a business expense. You might be dining with a client and talking business, trying to convince the person you are the right company to hire. You may be eating out to write a blog about the experience. As long as you discuss business during the meal or can consider the meal as part of a business necessity, you can deduct 50% of the meal and beverage costs. The idea is the meal has to fit the "ordinary and necessary" parameters.

Let's say you went on a run to pick up office supplies out of town because you live in a small town and it takes 30 miles to get to the office supply company. It took the entire day, so you needed food. You were working, therefore the meal counts.

If you dined out because you didn't want to go home for an hour and cook, before going back to the office, the meal would not count—unless—you discussed business with a partner, employee, or other person involved in the company.

Home-based Business Tax Deduction

If you run a business out of your home, you have tax deductions you can take. You do not want to miss these deductions at tax time, if you have enough to make it worthwhile. There is always a fine line between itemized deductions and standardized deductions that may be helpful or not. If you have minimal expenses with your business, then taking the itemized deductions is not worth it. You would pay out more in taxes than if you went with the standard deductions. You still file your home-based income, and TurboTax will add in any self-employed tax that needs to apply. However, you can deduct the home-office expenses as long as your home office. It is up to you to decide if the deductions are better being itemized or not.

First, you need to decide the percent of your home that your office takes up. For example, if your home office is 20% of the square footage of your home, you can deduct 20% of your bills for utilities, homeowner's insurance, HOA fees, security, repairs, maintenance, and other home related expenses like mortgage interest and property taxes.

Before you take the deduction or have your accountant take it, you need to understand the tax law.

You must use the office, only for business related work. It must be exclusive to your business- and business-related concepts. The office space must be separate from another area of the home. Now, you can use a divider, such as a room screen. The partition segments the office from home use areas. The amount of time you spend in your office is up to you, as long as each minute spent in the office area is for work only. For example, if you let your children into the office area and let them do their homework, you are no longer using the space "exclusively" for business and have violated the requirement. It means you cannot take the deductions.

Your family can come in and ask a question or you can take a personal phone call. The IRS says that as long as the interruptions are no more than would be at an actual commercial office building, they can occur.

Your home office has to be the office on file for the business and be the principal place you conduct your business. For employees who spend time at an office building part-time and work from home, they can still take the deduction as long as you are exclusive in the use of the office at home.

Note that if you have children and work from home, where your children are too young to be unsupervised, you can still take the deduction. You are considering part of the office as an in-workplace day care. Your office can also be used as storage, even if it is occasionally storing personal items. But your home must be the only place you work.

Calculating the home deduction is easier if you use the square footage. You should consider the square footage of your home and how much your office takes up. Let's say you have 250 square feet for your home, and your office is 8x8, which is 64 square feet. You would take 64 divided by 250 to gain the percentage. In this instance, the percentage is 25.6. You are allowed $5 per square feet, so 5 multiplied by 25.6 would give you the deduction amount, which is $128. These numbers are calculated using 2018 tax laws. It is imperative you check each year's tax laws to ensure nothing has changed about the home-based business deductions.

As mentioned above, you also have expenses you can deduct, such as utilities, property taxes, and more. It is important to learn the different options for these deductions.

A direct expense is one that is meant solely for the office, which means you deduct the entire amount. Long distance calls, painting the office, or a separate internet line for the office can all be a deduction.

Indirect expenses are those you will deduct based on percentage of office size. The electricity payment for the entire year is added up, and you can deduct the percentage of your office, meaning if 25.6 percent is your office space, you calculate the fees paid by 25.6 percent. Say you paid $400 for electricity, so 25.6 percent of that is the deducted amount or $102.

You can tell from the explanation that there are several opportunities to reduce the taxes owed by taking home-based business deductions. However, they can be complicated. Depending on the QuickBooks plan you might have TurboTax customer support to help you do your taxes. If you do not, it is something you can add with a TurboTax plan added to your QuickBooks plan.

The other choice is asking an accountant to review the information supplied and help you list all the deductions that apply. Thankfully, if you setup QuickBooks correctly for the type of business you have, its location, and you enter the bills you pay and reimbursements made for the deductions that count, it will be easier for you to ensure your accountant has everything they need to do your taxes correctly.

Remember, when we discussed adding bills and that you could reimburse yourself if you used a personal account for the purchase. Freelance and home-based businesses are where it truly matters that you do reimburse yourself for any personal payment for a business expense.

You could be missing deductions on your taxes because you are not an accountant or because you did not use an accounting software until now. Even if you are employed with a company and work from home, you might have missed some deductions in previous years. The good news is, you can usually make amendments and file for missed deductions. Again, it may take an accountant to go back through and do what needs to happen.

The above are the main deductions you do not want to forget. There are also some small business deductions to discuss.

Additional Deductions

- You can deduct expenses for cost of goods sold
- Capital expenses
- Some personal expenses

The cost of goods sold includes raw materials, freight, storage, cost of products, direct labor costs, and factory overhead. Note, the list includes additional deductions beyond what a freelance or self-employed worker at home would have.

Capital expenses include business start up costs, assets, and any improvements you make to your company.

When it comes to personal expenses, you have the option of making percentage deductions based on how frequently you use something for business versus personal. You get to divide the costs like the above discussion on utilities and your home office space.

If you are a freelancer, but you pay commissions, it is a deduction under the title "commissions." You need to record all commissions and show that the money was outgoing and was not straight income for you.

Companies that have employees may be able to deduct wagers and retirement plans. If you have a retirement plan because you set aside money on your own, it could be considered a business expense.

Any rental equipment or office rent is a deduction.

Interest paid, depending on the type of interest is still a deduction.

Taxes paid for assorted reasons may also be a deduction.

Insurance for the business, whether it is for the building, cars, or medical can be a deduction.

The above list is something you need to check on with the IRS each year. Tax laws change. Due to changes for small businesses, you may discover there are fewer deductions than in a previous year or if a new president vetoes laws, you might gain more deductions.

If you have any doubts or questions, seek an accountant to help you file your taxes. As a rule of thumb—keep all receipts whether you think something can be used as a deduction. You never know when you might need to provide the receipt as proof that you did or did not take deductions you were not supposed to.

CHAPTER 17

FILE MANAGEMENT SUGGESTIONS

Maintaining QuickBooks properly is not hard to do, if you keep up with the daily tasks. However, there are some things that are worth discussing to ensure you are using the various tasks and preventing issues later. For example, you need to backup your data, even if you use the online version.

Backing Up

You want to back up data anytime you use QuickBooks. Now, if you went into the program to look something up, it is not necessary to back up the information. However, if you went in and added a job, invoice, PO, created paychecks or anything else of importance—back it up.

1. Insert a disc, USB memory card, or other removable device into your computer.
2. Go to file.
3. Select "Copy File"
4. You have now backed everything up.

If you want to, you can back up your QuickBooks data online. You need a cloud storage account tied to QuickBooks. You can also link to QuickBooks storage options. There are usually fees for a business using online back up services. Check around to find the best cost for the options you obtain.

When you exit the program, it should ask you if you want to back up and how you wish to back up. There are prompts to follow for selecting the removable drive or backing up online. Simply follow the commands, name the file, and save.

Should any issues arise, you can get the data back.

●   Get the back up files on the removable drive or go to your online source.
●   Start QuickBooks and choose File
●   Click "Open or Restore Company"
●   Grab the file you want by clicking on it.
●   Tell QuickBooks where to pull from and click next.
●   You can then tell QuickBooks where you want the restore file to be saved.
●   Save

When you restore QuickBooks because something occurred to the data, you are replacing the last file it thinks you had. As long as you are restoring the information, you have nothing to worry about. If you forgot to back it up and an issue occurred, you will need to input everything again.

You do not want to forget to back up because you never know what might happen. Furthermore, you want the file to be in a separate device or location because your computer could crash and lose everything.

You will back up each time you add new information to ensure you have the most recent file in your back up location.

Portable Files

You have the option of creating a portable file for use by other people like your accountant, or even taking home some of the work from your main location. Working with portable files means you use a copy.

1. Go to File
2. Create Copy
3. Select the portable company file

To open it, the person will choose file, open, and restore, and be able to look at the file after following some on screen instructions.

Accountant Files

Your accountant does not need the entire back up of your QuickBooks program. Intuit understands this, so they created an accountant's copy option. You will follow the back up procedure, but this time select Accountant's Copy. Your accountant can take the file, review it, make changes, and you can import the changes.

Obviously, there are many features in QuickBooks you may need to use or want to know how to use periodically as your business grows or you make changes to certain functions you perform. With backing up the data for other people like accountants, you have audit and closing year options, but those details are something a basic guide will not cover.

Going to training or watching training videos is one way to learn those methods if you need them. All this guide wants you to know—is—you have many options to help you with housekeeping functions should you need them, but for most users the additional choices are not imperative.

CHAPTER 18

FIXED ASSETS AND VEHICLE INFORMATION

Business ownership may include fixed assets and vehicles, which you need to record as part of your assets for business wealth and potential depreciation deductions. This section will assess the details you need to know about assets and vehicles to help you with potential deductions and showing your company's financial health.

Fixed Assets

Fixed assets are those that are typically "fixed" in place, such as a building or machinery bolted to a floor. For the purpose of QuickBooks, any asset you have like furniture, equipment and vehicles can be added to the fixed asset list.

The list will track the costs, depreciations, and other valuable information for accounting. You can also calculate and record depreciations for tax returns and financial statements. Lastly, the lists are helpful in calculating and recording gains and losses that occur from disposed fixed assets. As you may be aware, at tax time you will list information about your assets, such as disposing of a computer that no longer works.

Your accountant will already have a list of these items, if you have worked with someone consistently for years. However, it is always helpful to add these things into QuickBooks to ensure you are reaping the benefits and to make it easier on your accountant. The way to save money—make it easy—your accountant can use everything from QuickBooks, pull reports and import it into a tax filing system. It saves time.

Now that you understand what fixed assets are and why you want to have a comprehensive list, it is time to discuss fixed assets accounting.

Fixed Assets Accounting

This type of accounting helps you keep a list of the assets you have, records the depreciation, and records the disposal of any thing you had. From the list, you will be able to update the journal entries when you sell or dispose of assets.

QUICKBOOKS

The setup is simple:

1. Under Lists, choose Fixed Asset Item List
2. Add an item
3. Name the asset
4. Enter the description of the item, basically you are choosing an account to tie it to.
5. Describe the purchase information
6. Save the details

Later you might wish to update the fixed asset.

7. Go to lists, fixed asset item list
8. Open the item to edit
9. Update the information

You now have everything you need for recording your assets, whether it is a building, computer, or other asset your business has.

It is time to look at tracking vehicle mileage, as this can have an impact on asset calculations.

Vehicles as Assets

Whether you use a personal vehicle or have multiple vehicles for company use, you need to understand the older they are the less valuable they become. You want to have a vehicle list and a way to record the miles. It is two-fold. You will use the depreciation information on taxes, plus you can deduct mileage as discussed in a previous section.

1. Go to list
2. Select Customer and Vendor Profile
3. Vehicle List
4. Click New
5. Enter the Vehicle
6. Save the information.

We already discussed entering vehicle mileage per employee. You also need to enter the beginning mileage as part of the asset details.

Each time a trip is made, you will go into the vehicle mileage area, choose the vehicle, enter the date and time, the starting mileage, and ending mileage, and attribute it to a job if you need to, then save the trip details.

Since vehicle mileage rates may change each year, you also want to know how to update the information for tax time. In Enter Vehicle Mileage, there is a mileage rate option, where you can put in the current rates and save. You are able to go to the IRS website to find the updated mileage information each year.

You should check twice a year regarding the mileage rates because sometimes the IRS updates the information more than once.

CHAPTER 19

SALES TAX CHANGES AND INFORMATION

While this is a guide for QuickBooks, it is truly relevant to how you use the software to help you with accounting. In 2018, a law was passed based on a court case between certain states and giant retailers. Previous to the new law, companies did not have to charge sales tax on items shipped out of city. The new law states, if you mail items out of city, you must charge sales tax for the city and state where the item is going, and any other special taxes like county or jurisdiction.

There are new rules based on the state you ship to and they are not the same across the board. Some states who have adopted the law say if you ship $250,000 worth of items out of state into their state or 1,000 plus packages, you need to start charging sales tax.

The changes require you to spend more time on calculating sales tax for items shipped. There are handy websites that will help you figure out what you need to charge. These websites allow you to enter the address items are shipped to and will give you the tax code, plus the breakdown of the sales tax you will calculate.

The information you gain from the sales tax website can be entered on your invoices. Going back to the point of creating your invoices, you will enter tax information, such as whether the company is tax exempt or what tax you need to charge. Once you have the vendor information, you can keep it in QuickBooks to ensure you pull it up each time you create a new invoice.

Out of State Rules

Your local government page will help you find the new rules outlining whether the states you are shipping to have passed any sales tax law changes and adopted the new rules.

Looking by state, you will see what rules you need to follow.

It is important to keep track of the items you have shipped and the amount it totals to—you will want to prove why or why you did not collect tax—if you are audited.

Small businesses that rarely ship items out of their state are largely unconcerned with the tax law changes. Let's discuss the bookstore example. A person called the store, they saw a book when they visited over the summer and want to buy it. The book is $25.00, and shipping is $3.60. It is going to a state you did not ship to previously, therefore according to state rules, you don't have to charge taxes. But, let's say the next person is in Texas and you have shipped twenty items in the last six months to people in Texas. Now, you need to review the rules to see the amount set for charging tax. You may not qualify for the dollar amount, but how about the number of packages sent? It is an "or" situation, so if you send over $250,000 worth or you send 100 items, you may need to charge tax (this is an example and not reflecting any state).

In State Laws

If your state has adopted the sales tax law amendment, you are now responsible for charging sales tax to anyone you ship to in your state, regardless of the "out of state" rules. Some states are still ironing out the details. They may have a projected date for when you need to adopt the new rules, or you may need to be incompliance now. Check with your accountant and read the state rules.

There are two things you will want to do if you need to start charging sales tax when you ship in state.

1. POS updates

2. QuickBooks

If your point of sale system is part of QuickBooks, you can amend the sales tax information, as necessary. When you have QuickBooks for accounting purposes only, check to see if you can amend your sales tax to cover all parameters or if you need to manually enter the data when you make sales.

Many of the newer point of sales systems allow you to set up the most frequent sales taxes you are going to use to make it easier on you. You still use the online sales tax website to discover the code and the taxes to charge, but you get to keep it in the system to prevent yourself from working harder than you need to when you ship things.

For sales tax reports, make sure you are adding new sales tax information for each sales tax you charge. The reports are essential when it comes to filing your monthly sales tax payments.

Sales Tax Payments

In previous sections we discussed tax liabilities. Now we are going to go in-depth with the sales tax discussion.

Sales tax is collected each time you make a sale. You charge it using the POS system or when you create a receipt in QuickBooks. If you use QuickBooks, then you know the information is being saved and you can go into

311

reports, create the sales tax report, and use that for your tax payments.

However, if you use two separate systems, you will need to update QuickBooks or use a different method for calculating the sales tax. Given that you have an option to record the monthly sales tax by reconciling your daily income split into the items purchased and tax collected, you will find it easy to create the report.

Even better, is sales tax payments are now made online. You are required to file the sales tax information and send the payment via electronic methods. If you do not pay your sales tax by the 15th of each month for the previous month, there is a hefty penalty. Do not let yourself get into a situation where you pay this horrible penalty. Due to the online system, you can import information from approved data sheets, such as sales tax reports created by QuickBooks.

By now, you should have a log in, unless you are opening a new business. Go to the state sales tax website, create a log in with username and password, and outline your company details.

If necessary, call your accountant to help you get this set up. During the setup phase, set up the payment method you are going to use, such as a direct electronic transfer from your bank account where the sales tax is deposited.

Using the month end reports, calculate the deposit information sans the sales tax paid. Any paid outs;

mailed out of city and out of state information, and other information requested by the tax website should be entered. The online document will calculate what you owe, and you can follow the steps to make a payment.

Since the tutorial is about QuickBooks, the details on filing Sales Tax are not complete. They are straightforward, and your state is on hand if you have questions. Once the payments are made record them in QuickBooks as an expense, so you can reconcile your account correctly for the ACH payment that came out of your bank account.

CHAPTER 20

QUICKBOOKS TIPS

You have made it this far in the QuickBooks guide. Should you have a handle on most QuickBooks functions, but want some quick tips—this is the place to be reading.

Work Flow Tips for Bookkeeping

To make life easier as the bookkeeper for a business, there are tasks you should keep on top of based on your job description. People who come in once a week to work as a bookkeeper may not find all the details here, helpful. But if you are an in-house bookkeeper consider the suggestions.

- Daily – enter money in and out transactions.
- Daily – send estimates and sales forms to clients
- Daily – enter new assets and liabilities

314

- Daily – check incoming bank transactions
- Weekly – look for unpaid invoices and bills (accounts receivable and payable)
- Weekly – add and edit any new vendor and customer details
- Weekly – add and edit services and product information
- Weekly – monitor the bank information
- Monthly – reconcile your bank accounts
- Monthly – run profit and loss statements from the previous month
- Review any problems
- Quarterly – check in with your accountant and create the accountant report

These task tips help you keep on top of the tasks, so the jobs are easier. What could take an hour may only take a few minutes each due to the upkeep you have. There are also fewer potential mistakes when you are entering on a daily, weekly, or monthly basis regarding the tasks.

The above is also a suggested timetable that may not fit your business model or job description. You have to decide what works for you and your company.

Freelancers may have fewer updates on a daily basis due to closed service orders and payments made. As an example, a person may be paid once a month for an entire months' work, which is where tracking the jobs is important and ensuring the freelancer invoices for all work before the monthly cut off date.

Designing your Business Model

QuickBooks is wonderful because it has numerous features for various business models. Yet, you still need to incorporate as much information as possible to design the business model and make QuickBooks as useful as it can possibly be.

Freelancers and home-based self-employed individuals may benefit from the freelance version or the next step up, but the way to benefit is to ensure you create a business model and schedule of tasks for what you do and the time frame it happens in. A good rule is to enter as much information as possible into QuickBooks and ignore what you find is not essential.

Custom Fields

QuickBooks is designed on the premise that your small business will have similar classes or categories for items based on tax details. Accountants need specific information for deductions and income allocations. Creating custom fields may be unnecessary or may not help you.

On tax forms, there are places for "other" income or expenses. You are required to be specific in your description when you use the "other" category. You can also create your own, so you show the specific business income or expenses that do not fit in the generalized tax categories.

Should you find it necessary to create custom fields, you are more apt to see a drop-down list to help you. However, you can also add "other" and customize something special. Whether you need it for taxes, or it is something to help you see a difference in a QuickBooks report, at least you do have the option of adding custom fields.

You do so by going into the area that is suited to the custom creation, such as Vendor, class, and adding a new category type.

User Roles and Permissions

There are times when you want admin, for administrator, where you are able to perform all functions in QuickBooks, such as when you are the only user. For companies who have multiple employees using the timesheet functions, you will want to create user roles and permissions.

Under Company, go to Users, Set up users, and Roles.

- Look at the roles list tab to see if there is a role that fits your employee.

- Create a role if necessary.
- Click edit to add more functionality or take permissions away.
- Save the changes made.

Now, you have a way for other users to access what they need to do, without being able to view confidential business documents. As you are aware, QuickBooks is designed to work with a certain number of users and may function as the service or sales software for your company. You want permissions restricted for the level your employee is, while retaining higher permissions for those of increased status in the company.

Transaction History

QuickBooks helps you maintain information and sometimes you might have trouble finding specific transactions, but for one reason or another you need to review the details. You can do so, by going into reports, selecting transaction history, and filling out the prompts it provides. It will help you find a transaction, even if it has been a year or more since you made the sale.

Linking Email

Another helpful feature of QuickBooks is linking with various accounts, including your email. Many vendors and clients use email to avoid paper waste. You will find you are sending out emails with invoices versus faxes, calling, or seeing a vendor in person. Linking your email is helpful because you can send the invoice, reminders, and credit memos directly to the company via email. QuickBooks will link with Outlook, Yahoo, Gmail, and other email operators. You do not have to import your contacts, you just tell QuickBooks you want to email something, and you will go to the email to attach the invoice through QuickBooks.

CONCLUSION

Congratulations you have reached the end of the guide. You have this guide at your disposal for whenever you have questions, forget how to do a task, or need to learn something you glossed over in the previous study.

Use this guide as a means of helping you learn QuickBooks, as well as feeling confident that it's the right decision to add it to your company. It's understandable that you might have begun work as a freelancer and your company took off, so now you need bookkeeping and accounting software. You may have bought an older business and want to upgrade its capabilities. No matter what situation you are in, you have the option of bringing in QuickBooks as a new or existing company.

If you are ever unsure of how to launch the program, contact QuickBooks or have your accountant stop by for the installation. Established companies will have more of a transition than someone starting a new business. It might require more time and help.

You also have training classes and self-paced learning experience to help you become an expert on the functionality of QuickBooks.

When you start using QuickBooks, it is best to use every option it has that applies to your company. You do not want to start using a portion of the software now and then try to add more functions later. For example, you might set up the bare minimum for writing employee checks, but later you want to use the full functionality. Going backwards is more difficult than if you set it up right the first time.

Thank you for purchasing this guide and hopefully you have found it helpful to your business needs.